The Hyles Sunday School Manual

by
Dr. Jack Hyles,
Pastor, First Baptist Church, Hammond, Indiana

Sword of the Lord Publishers
Murfreesboro, Tennessee 37130

ISBN 0-87398-373-4

Printed and bound in The United States of America

Dedication

Dedicated to the departmental superintendents of the Sunday school of the First Baptist Church of Hammond, Indiana,

Mrs. Richard Barr
Mrs. Lowell Burnside
Mrs. Johnny Colsten
Mrs. C. W. Fisk
Mrs. Tom McKinney
Mrs. Raymond Newton
Mrs. Reginald Plopper
Mrs. Robert Plopper
Mrs. Alvin Rice
Mrs. Walter Ruskowski
Mrs. Lewis Shoaf
Mrs. Glen Smith
Mrs. Lindsay Terry
Mrs. Martin Waechter

and to the over three hundred teachers and officers who have faithfully and diligently tested and proved the workability of the methods advanced in this Manual.

Pictured above is the Sunday school of the First Baptist Church of Hammond, Indiana, which averaged over 3400 during 1968 and which for the last three months of the year averaged over 4000.

TABLE OF CONTENTS

Foreword

"How many did you have in Sunday school last Sunday?" "What is your Sunday school averaging now?" These and many similar questions can be heard at conventions, in fellowship meetings, and at many other places where pastors convene and converse. Such questions remind us that the Sunday school is the number one criterion by which we judge the success of our churches. Hence, I felt impressed to add *The Hyles Sunday School Manual* to The Hyles Manual Series. Methods and materials presented herein come from the author's experiences of over twenty years of pastoring churches whose Sunday schools have ranged in attendance from 7 to 4700.

1. The Organization of the Sunday School

Proper organization is essential to any thriving institution. It is important, however, to emphasize the word "proper." Too much organization can add weights to the Sunday school. Too little organization can prevent its operating with peak efficiency. The following is a discussion aimed at providing just the right amount of organization for Sunday school growth.

1. *The Church.* The Sunday school is "the church teaching." It is a dangerous thing for Sunday school not to be considered the church. I have been in churches where the pastor does not attend Sunday school. Believe it or not, in some rare instances the church even charges the Sunday school rent for the use of the buildings. In many cases church leaders and officials have no part in the Sunday school. I have known deacon chairmen who attended no Sunday school class whatsoever. The Sunday school should be considered a part of the church program. The entire church should consider it a vital hour. In some cases the church approves all of the Sunday school officers. In other cases the church empowers the pastor or a committee to do so. At any rate, the election of a teacher should not be in the hands of a class. A class should never divorce itself from the program of the church. The church should promote the Sunday school, and the Sunday school should promote the church. Truly, they are one! The entire time from the beginning of the Sunday school hour until the end of the morning service should be considered all one church service by God's people.

2. *The Pastor.* There are several words in the Bible for "pastor." One is the word "bishop" which means "over-

10   THE HYLES SUNDAY SCHOOL MANUAL

seer." This means the pastor should oversee the entire church program. He should take a vital interest in the Sunday school. He should definitely be the leader whether behind the scenes or before the people. For nearly a quarter of a century I have directed the work of the Sunday school in each of my five pastorates. For all of these years I have led in the conducting of the Teachers' and Officers' Meeting, the teaching of the lesson to my teachers, the planning of the promotional activities, and every other phase of the Sunday school program.

3. *The Sunday School Superintendent.* This office should not be filled by one who simply has the gift of gab, a winning personality, or is popular in the church. It should be filled by the one who knows the most about Sunday school and is the best leader of the Sunday school. In many cases, this should be the pastor. Some churches find this office should be filled by one of the assistant pastors. In some areas churches have educational directors and this office carries with it the superintendent of the Sunday school In other churches a layman is Sunday school superintendent. Which of the above is chosen for the job is dependent upon one thing and one thing only: Who is the best Sunday school leader of the group?

The Sunday school superintendent should oversee the entire work of the Sunday school along *WITH* the pastor. He should be the dynamic inspiration behind the enlistment of workers, the choosing of the departmental superintendents, the keeping of the records, and every other phase of the Sunday school program.

4. *Departmental Superintendent.* This is the key person of the Sunday school as far as promoting attendance is concerned. Such a person should be responsible for supervising and directing the entire work of the department. He should be a good executive, able to inspire his workers and work with others. His main duties would be planning and conducting the opening assembly for the department, organizing the department properly, encouraging the teachers to do better jobs, inspiring and leading the department with enthusiasm and growth, seeing that adequate provision is made for all the work of the department, filling vacancies when teachers are unavoidably absent, and in general,

overseeing the work of the department. Perhaps the most important of these responsibilities is the promoting of the attendance and the inspiring of the teachers to do the same. When the pastor and/or Sunday school superintendent lead in a spring or fall program or any kind of Sunday school drive, he should have the kind of departmental superintendents who will see to it that their departments grow and who can instill in their workers and pupils the desire to do a better job for God.

It is my conviction that many churches have too many departments and therefore, too many departmental superintendents. Not just any person can be a departmental superintendent. It requires a rare combination of wisdom, knowledge, and zeal.

5. *The Teacher.* Rather than the teacher being subservient to the superintendent, I like to think of the teacher and the superintendent simply working in different areas. The superintendent oversees the work of the departmental assembly and promotion, while the teacher teaches the Word of God and builds the class.

The pastor is what the general is to an army. The Sunday school superintendent is what the colonel is to the general. The departmental superintendents are company commanders, and the teachers are squad leaders. We will not dwell long here for much of this book is given to the instructions, enlistment, and qualifications of the teachers.

6. *The Assistant Superintendent.* Sometimes this is a duty of a staff member. When it is, it involves the work of increasing attendance, leading the visitation program, and substituting for the superintendent in case of emergency. Usually this office can be filled on a part-time basis by one of the teachers. The decision that is made should be based upon the local situation.

7. *General Teachers.* I do not like having substitute teachers. We have found it much more helpful to have what we call "general teachers." In a department with fifteen classes two people could be chosen as general teachers. They would be considered as much a part of the department as the regular teachers. They would come to the weekly Teachers' and Officers' Meeting and would come to the department each Sunday prepared to teach. They would

be available to teach when and if needed. There are many miscellaneous duties that they could perform in addition to substituting for teachers as an emergency (or in some cases, delinquency). The general teacher should be treated with all of the respect of a regular teacher and should be chosen and enlisted in the same manner.

8. *Class Organization.* In our Sunday school at the First Baptist Church of Hammond we have our classes organized, and yet this organization is a very loose one. The average class simply has a president, vice-president, and secretary. The secretary cares for the class records; the president assists the teacher in class planning and presides on Sunday morning; and the vice-president presides in the absence of the president. The theory of this is that the main duty of every Christian should be soul winning and visitation, and nothing should excuse a Christian from such. Often the holding of offices which have nothing to do with soul winning become substitutes for the big thing. That big thing, of course, is reaching people for the Lord Jesus Christ. No amount of organization, no job regardless of its importance, and no duty regardless of its benevolence, will substitute for the carrying out of the Great Commission, which, simply stated, is soul winning!

In a children's class organized this loosely the class is started by the teacher standing up and warmly welcoming the pupils and visitors. The teacher then very enthusiastically and courteously introduces the president who stands, adds his greetings, calls the class to order, and asks someone to pray. The class president then turns to the teacher and introduces him for the introduction of the visitors. The teacher, who has already gotten the visitors' names and interesting facts about them before the class started, rises to welcome the visitors. The visitors' names are called, and interesting statements are made concerning them. After the visitors are properly introduced the teacher turns it back to the president. The president then makes the necessary announcements concerning the weekday activities of the class and any special events for the class in the future. He may add his greeting to the visitors, and then very courteously he introduces the teacher. The teacher follows with the lesson and closes the class.

In classes for older children and adults the above procedure is also recommended except that the president is in charge of all preliminaries. This would apply only to small, medium-sized classes. In a case of a large auditorium class taught by the pastor, perhaps he would recognize the visitors and make the announcements. In small classes, however, especially for those of older children, it might be wise that more time and duties be given to the president in order to train teachers and leaders for the future.

Many Sunday schools, however, desire more organization than this for their Sunday schools. We suggest the following offices and duties:

(1) *President.* Since the secret to any organization is its leadership, the president should be careful to keep the following things in mind:

a. *Faithfulness.* The president should be one who is always present. By this it is not meant that the president should merely be willing to be faithful. Certainly no office should be given to one in order to make him faithful. The president should be one who is already faithful to all of the activities of the church.

b. *Neatness in appearance.* In many cases the first impression a visitor will get is that given by the president. Hence, a president should set an example. The president should be one who dresses appropriately and is careful about such things as shoes, fingernails, hair, etc. The first impression should be a good one.

c. *In adult classes the president should be able to teach in case of emergency.* If the teacher suddenly becomes ill or is called away for an emergency, the class will not be seriously handicapped if the president is prepared. Not only is it a good idea for the president to be able to teach, but he should be prepared to do so every Sunday if needed. It may be that he will never be needed, but he himself will benefit from the extensive study of the lesson, even if he is not used as a teacher.

d. *The president should preside with efficiency.* The

Lord's work should be done properly. Nothing slipshod, haphazard, or halfhearted should be given to God. Certainly no moderator in any secular endeavor should preside with more efficiency than the president of a Sunday school class. He should know what he is doing and it should be obvious to the class. The slipshod way in which God's work is often done is absolutely tragic. We usually say that God's work is the most important in the world. Careless behavior, planning, and operating of God's work would lead a bystander to believe that God's work is not very important in the minds of those who lead. How tragic!

e. *The president should present the teacher each week.* A good introduction is very important to a speaker and oftentimes can spell the difference between success and failure. If the president would say something like, "We thank God for our teacher who has prepared something for our hearts today. Let us pray for him as he brings the lesson from God's Word," it would be of inestimable value to the teacher and hence to the class.

f. *The president should constantly keep in touch with the other class officers, being sure that their duties are performed in a Christian and efficient manner.* Some classes find it wise to have a brief, thirty-second report from each officer each week. If this does not increase the total time taken on business to four or five minutes, it may be done with efficiency and impressiveness.

g. *The president should plan a monthly get-together for the class.* This meeting should be highly planned and should be a combination of business and pleasure. He may work with the teacher in this endeavor as is discussed in the chapter, "Weekday Duties of the Teacher."

h. *The president could join the teacher in greeting the class members as they enter the classroom.* Certainly the president should be friendly and hospitable, and should make each person feel needed, wanted, and welcome.

(2) *Vice-president.* In a class that is highly organized the vice-president should do the following:

a. *Be a ready substitute for the president in case of his absence.* Because of this, the vice-president should possess a satisfactory amount of presidential qualities such as neatness, friendliness, hospitality, etc.

b. *The vice-president should be in charge of the visitation program of the class.* He should promote visitation, lead the class in a special visitation method, keep a prospect list. He is the number one person as far as the enlargement of the class is concerned.

c. *The vice-president should be able to care for the records in case the secretary is absent.* In other words, this office is a combination of vice-president and vice-secretary.

In our generation we have found the importance of choosing a good vice-president. When President Kennedy was assassinated, we realized immediately that our country was in the hands of one not previously chosen to be a president, rather a vice-president. Hence, the vice-president in any organization should always be a capable one.

(3) *Secretary.*

a. *The secretary should pass out envelopes at the door.* If offering envelopes are used, they can be received as they enter the class. This would allow the secretary to add a warm smile and even a friendly handshake to that of the teacher and president.

b. *The secretary should be sure that each visitor and new member has a visitor's card and a new member's slip.*

c. *If the class is divided into groups, the secretary should present each group captain with an absentee list.* Since the secretary works with the records, he should alert those who lead in the visitation program with a list of the delinquent members.

d. *The secretary should keep the class money and give a monthly report.*

e. *Perhaps the secretary could give a brief report at the end of class.* This report could tell the class members the highlights of the day's statistics. It should be understood that this report, as all reports, should be an optimistic one. It should not be a time of scolding, but a time of inspiration.

f. *The secretary should keep an accurate set of records.* It is very important that all cards and records be kept up to date and accurate. Numbers are very important in the Bible. Occasionally someone will minimize the importance of numbers in God's work, and in most cases, their numbers are very minimal. We are reminded of the feeding of the five thousand, the hundred and twenty in the upper room, and the three thousand people saved on Pentecost. One book in the Bible is called "Numbers." Hence, God places His significance on numbers, for a number represents a person, and we should try to reach as many people as possible.

The job of the secretary should not be taken lightly. In our present board of deacons we have one of the most efficient secretaries that I have known. It is amazing how much the work is aided by such a dedicated secretary.

(4) *Group Captain.* Some classes are divided into groups with a group captain over each group. Sometimes this is done for visitation purposes, sometimes for social purposes, or other reasons. Whatever the reason, it is often used very successfully. Naturally the success of the group rests upon the shoulders of the group captain.

a. *In a medium-sized class one group captain for each ten members is advisable.* Now, of course, this would not be true in every case. In some large auditorium classes, a group captain may even have a hundred. In such a case he would

have to organize his group so as to enlist others
to help him in the contacting of absentees and
prospects. It is thought, however, that one
group captain could very well captain ten members and do all of the visiting himself.

b. *The group captain should be a pastor to his
members.* He should be willing to offer counsel,
visit hospitals, pray for the sick, etc. One of
the great reasons for organization is the delega-
tion of responsibility. The larger a church and
Sunday school becomes the more people must
enter into the pastoring work. Certainly a group
captain can be a great help here.

c. *The group captain should call the faithful members regularly.* This could be just a brief phone
call of a social nature to remind the faithful
people that they are not neglected, overlooked
or unappreciated.

d. *The group captain should contact all absentees.*
In smaller classes the teacher can care for this.
For classes large enough to demand division
into groups, a group captain should certainly
contact all absentees each week.

e. *A group captain should keep in touch with the
associate members.* An associate member is a
class member who is working elsewhere, but
would otherwise be present in the class. Associate members could be Sunday school teachers,
departmental superintendents, and other office
holders throughout the Sunday school. Oftentimes these people are overlooked in social activities, yet they do have such a need. A group
captain should be in contact with these people informing them of class parties, etc.

f. *The group captain should remember birthdays,
illnesses, and special events.* Birthday greetings
should be sent by the group captains. The
sick should be visited, and special occasions
should be remembered.

g. *The group captain should let his group be aware
of his appreciation.* He is a go-between between

the teacher and the member. In a real sense, he represents the teacher. He is to the class what the assistant pastor oftentimes is to the church. He helps solve problems, calm disputes, and keeps the class wholesome and happy.

(5) *Sunshine Chairman.* Though often called by other titles the sunshine chairman is a very important person in a well-organized class. The duties evolve around the title — simply the bringing of sunshine into darkened lives.

   a. *The sunshine chairman should offer food and other help in times of need.* This would include the care for the poor, the carrying of food to a family who has lost a loved one, the sending of flowers to funerals, the remembering of birthdays, etc. Especially is the sunshine chairman an important person when the class is not divided into groups. If the class is divided into groups, there may be no need whatsoever for the sunshine chairman.

   b. *The sunshine chairman should keep the room neat.* Once again his job is to bring sunshine into the lives of the pupils. He could arrive early on Sunday to prepare the classroom in such an attractive way that the entire day of the pupils will be made brighter.

There are many other things that the sunshine chairman could do. Simply think of anything that could bring sunshine or joy into the life of a member and you have thought of a duty for this officer.

(6) *Mission Chairman.* Of course, when we think of the word "mission," we immediately think of foreign missions, and around this ministry evolve the basic responsibilities of the mission chairman.

   a. *The mission chairman should correspond with the missionaries.* When letters are received from the mission field, they should be read to the class. In some cases the letters could be copied and each member could receive the information firsthand.

   b. *The mission chairman should encourage the*

class to correspond with the missionaries. He should play "cupid" between the missionary and the class member, doing all that he can to keep them aware of each other.

c. *He should keep a list of the missionaries' birthdays and certainly should never forget them.* He then should forward this information to each class member. How wonderful it is for a person on the foreign field to receive many birthday cards from home! How often they are forgotten! It is the duty of the mission chairman to see that this is not done.

d. *The mission chairman should keep the class informed with facts concerning all missionaries.* The class should know something about the activities and even the personal lives of those who represent them on the foreign mission field. When this is done, missionaries become "live" people and foreign mission work becomes alive.

e. *The mission chairman should remember the missionaries on special occasions.* Anniversaries, birthdays, Christmas, and other special occasions should be remembered by the Sunday school. It is the duty of the mission chairman to see that this is done.

f. *The mission chairman should lead the class in a class mission project.* This can be done by writing the missionaries and seeking information concerning their needs. Once these needs are known the class should choose a need for its own project. Such projects can put new life and new direction into a Sunday school class. It would certainly encourage the hearts and aid the work of many missionaries.

(7) *Social Chairman.* People are sociable creatures and demand social life. Such needs can be provided by the teacher, the president, or in some cases, a special officer called the "social chairman." When such an office is needed, the following social activities should be planned by the social chairman.

a. *A monthly class meeting.* This provides a regular meeting to which the class members can look with anticipation. It builds comradeship and offers a tremendous substitute for other organizations which Christians should not join. This class meeting does not have to be elaborately planned, and it does not have to be lengthy, just long enough and well planned enough to make the class members feel brotherly and sisterly toward each other.

b. *A quarterly social.* Once each three months the social chairman should prepare a very pleasant time of social life for the class members. This does not have to be a stage production, but it should be well planned and well prepared. Here the class can learn to laugh together.

c. *A gigantic family party annually.* This is the big event of the class year. The families should be invited and it should be something toward which each member would look with delight. A nice banquet could be planned or a big picnic would also fill this need. Some classes have a huge Christmas party. Whenever it is or whatever it is does not matter. What matters is that the class members should have a time of learning to know each other better as well as a time of meeting.

(8) *Songleader.* Every class that meets without having had a departmental assembly should have a songleader. If the class is a part of a department, then the department should have a songleader. People like to sing, and many people sing well. This is a part in which every person can share, and through which each person can express his own emotions. A good songleader can certainly be used to stir enthusiasm. Sometimes the superintendent is the best songleader available. At other times the teacher could perhaps lead the singing. It is better, however, to find someone other than the aforementioned so as to spread responsibilities of the department.

(9) *A Pianist.* In each department there should be a responsible person who plays the piano well. In

addition to playing for the department the pianist could be used in preparing and arranging special numbers for the department or the class. In some cases this should be done by the songleader; in other cases, the pianist would be more qualified.

2. The Division of Departments

In the building of a Sunday school and in the training of children and young people, it is vitally important that the proper division be made concerning age, sex, etc.

Age Division

1. *Nursery*—birth through age three should be divided into at least three different divisions:
   (1) *Bed babies*
   (2) *Toddlers* (The child becomes a toddler as soon as he is no longer left in the crib or bed. He remains a toddler until his second birthday.)
   (3) *Two- and three-year-olds.* In this discussion we will say very little about the organization and layout of a church nursery. We will center our attention on the teachable ages of two and up. In the author's book, *The Hyles Church Manual,* there is an entire chapter given to the church nursery. Any Sunday school superintendent or pastor would be wise to read carefully the suggestions contained in this chapter. We will limit our suggestions in this discussion by simply saying that the nicest facilities in the church should be given to the nurseries, and unlimited attention, care, planning, preparation, etc., should be given to the nursery facilities.

   When a child reaches the age of two, however, he is ready to begin his Sunday school life. (In some cases he may approach this era a little younger.) In larger churches and in smaller churches, if at all possible, it is best to divide the two-year-olds from the three-year-olds. The younger a person is, the more changes are made in his life within a year, and the more important it is that he be separated from those of different ages.

It is wise on the nursery level to promote a child on his birthday. In other words, when a child reaches his second birthday, he should immediately go into the nursery department where he can be taught. For all Sunday school pupils above nursery age, Promotion Day is on one particular Sunday each year.

The Sunday following the child's second birthday he is taken to his new surroundings. This means that the two- and three-year-old departments may be small on Promotion Day, but they will continue to grow throughout the entire year.

2. *Beginners — ages four and five*

This department completes the preschool children. In smaller churches perhaps they would have to be together in the same department. It is advisable, however, when at all possible, to have different departments (or at least different classes) for each age — four and five. Up through the age of five it is best to have each department in one large room, with each teacher sitting at a table with his or her class.

3. *Primary — ages six and seven or grades one and two*

In some cases the primaries include the eight-year-olds and the 3rd grade. We have found it best, however, to limit the primaries to two grades, and we much prefer the divisions by grades in school rather than by age. Using this method the pupils are more likely to know each other since they are together most of the week at school.

Now when we come to the primary age we find it necessary to divide the boys from the girls, and to give each class its own private room or area. The girls and boys meet together for an opening assembly and then the boys go to classes taught by men and the girls go to classes taught by ladies. From the first grade through high school all boys are taught by men in our Sunday school. Also, all girls are taught by ladies. Most churches will find it necessary to have one primary department with several classes. Larger churches, however, would be very wise to have two primary departments—one for the first grade and another for the second grade with several classes in each department. When a child reaches the first grade he then enters the first time into a department where the assembly is for all the children, but his class is taught in a private room, and the lecture-type teaching method is used.

4. *Juniors — grades three through six*

The departmental and class setup is the same as the primaries. The smaller church may find it necessary to have all of the juniors in one department, but in such cases the division of classes should definitely be made by grade. In other words, all the juniors of the church may meet together for an opening assembly, then there could be a class for 3rd-grade boys and a class for 3rd-grade girls, a class for 4th-grade boys and a class for 4th-grade girls, etc.

When at all possible, it is highly desirable to have a department for each grade and then the classes may be divided into smaller groups in the same grade.

5. *Junior High — grades seven and eight*

Again it is desirable to have a department for each grade, but its importance is not as great as that of the beginner, primary and junior-age departments. It is very satisfactory to have one Junior High Department with the classes divided according to grades. Still in larger churches, two departments would be more desirable.

6. *High School — grades nine through twelve*

This can be all one department with class division by grades, two departments with class division by grades, or four departments with class division by grades. Of course, each department should be divided into classes.

7. *Geographical division of classes*

My present pastorate is located in a downtown section. People come from far and near to our Sunday school. Because of this, we find it very helpful to divide the classes by geographical locations. In other words, the members of each class live in the same area. There are several advantages to this. One is that the teacher's visitation is helped greatly. More visits can be made in a given amount of time because there is less traveling involved between visits.

Then, too, the class members are more likely to know each other, for they probably attend the same school if they live in the same area.

8. *Relaxing the visitors' grade level by one year*

In churches which are able to offer a department for each grade level, enlisting of prospects becomes a problem. For example, I have an eight-year-old daughter. If she can invite only third graders to her department, many of her best friends will not go to the same department when they visit with her in the Sunday school. Because of this we have found it advisable to start the year on Promotion Day with only third graders attending the third grade department. During the year, however, we allow the workers and pupils to invite and enlist boys and girls from one grade under and from one grade over their particular grade level. For example, my eight-year-old daughter, who is in the third grade, can invite second graders and fourth graders to her department. This gives a department three grades to work on instead of one. This, of course, is limited to visitors and new members to Sunday school. She cannot invite those who are from other departments in our Sunday school. This rule applies to all grades through high school. At the end of the year when Promotion Day comes, we once again readjust the entire Sunday school. Each person is "promoted" to his proper department and repeats the same procedure. We have found this plan very beneficial in the growing of a department and in the increasing of the attendance.

At this writing the departmental division of the First Baptist Church is as follows:

Nursery 1 - bed babies
Nursery 2 - toddlers
Nursery 3 - 2 years
Nursery 4 - 3 years
Beginner 1 - 4 years
Beginner 2 - 5 years
Primary 1 - 1st grade
Primary 2 - 2nd grade
Junior 1 - 3rd and 4th grades
Junior 2 - 5th grade
Junior 3 - 6th grade

Junior High 1 - 7th grade
Junior High 2 - 8th grade
High School 1 - 9th and 10th grades
High School 2 - 11th and 12th grades

3. The Division of Adult Classes

When we come to the division of the adult classes and departments we find great diversion and differences of opinion. We will list several of them along with their advantages and disadvantages.

1. *The Adult Auditorium Class*

Many of America's largest churches use this plan. It is a very simple one, for all of the adults come to the auditorium and are taught by one teacher. Usually the teacher is the pastor. In some cases, it is simply a large Sunday school class with a Sunday school class atmosphere. Variations of the large auditorium class range all the way from making it like a preaching service with a choir, special music, invitation, etc., to a simple lecture-type class session. In some cases no attempt is made for organization, registration, or even a class roll. There is simply the taking of the offering and the head count. Some Sunday schools have found it profitable to divide the class into groups with group captains overseeing the attendance and growth of the class. Some of the much larger churches have paid staff members who are hired to see that each group grows and that absentees are contacted.

The great advantage of such a plan is the tremendous savings involved as far as buildings and space are concerned. In a church that runs 500 in such a class, it would be necessary to spend hundreds of thousands of dollars for a building that would adequately house small departments and classes for the same number of people.

Then there is also a safety factor involved in such a setup. Certainly the class has a qualified teacher, and since the pastor usually is that teacher, he has no fear concerning what is taught to his adults. He can be confident of their loyalty.

This plan also enables the husbands and wives to be together in Sunday school. It enables the adults to stay in one room during the entire Sunday school and preaching services.

On the other hand, the plan has its limitations. Most churches have more than one teacher qualified to teach adults. Hence these talents are not utilized.

Then there is a problem concerning the social life of this class. Class socials for such a large class are difficult to plan. Many churches compensate for this by dividing the class into groups and having group socials and group activities.

Much care should be taken in the utilization of such a plan to make the stranger and the new member feel a part of the class. He does not have the closeness nor the personal touch provided by a smaller class, but this can be overcome by proper organization by the class leadership.

All in all, I feel that this plan should be given some consideration by many churches. The small growing church which has limited space should consider the auditorium adult class. The church that is growing so fast that its building cannot keep up with its attendance would find this plan a definite asset. The young church with a limited number of qualified workers no doubt should give consideration to this plan. Though no two churches have the same problems or needs, and though this author feels that no one solution is the answer for the problems of all churches, many great churches in America, both small and large, are finding success in growth through the use of the large auditorium class for adults.

2. *The Grading of Adults*

In contrast to the aforementioned auditorium class is the complete grading of the adults into departments and classes. Such a plan divides all of the adults into as many departments as space will permit. These departments are divided by age and the classes within the departments are divided by age. Some churches go so far as to have the departments with as few as fifty enrolled. In such a department there would be five classes with ten members each. This enables a large church to have many adult departments with scores of classes. Advocates of this plan would argue convincingly that the absentees can be visited regularly and more personal attention can be given to each pupil. However, this is not the only advantage to such a plan. More people are put to work. The class is more intimate and, consequently, more friendly. Most visitors do not feel as conspicuous in such a class. There is more opportunity to ask questions. It is easier to have group discussion. The members are with those near their same age, etc.

The graded adult plan also has its weaknesses. It requires the church to build nearly twice as many educational buildings and oftentimes tempts the church to give the best facilities to the adults, leaving the leftovers to the children.

There are few churches who have enough qualified workers to give one to each ten adults, and therefore, this often results in inferior teaching on the adult level. Let us never forget, the purpose of the Sunday school is to teach the Word of God. This should not be lost in the forest of social life, personal friendliness, etc. Those who oppose this plan will point to this as its most glaring weakness.

There is one more weakness, however, that should be emphasized. In the graded adult plan the person has one choice and only one concerning his class and teacher. Since he has to go to the department and class for his particular age, he has little choice. He must either (1) like the teacher, (2) not like the teacher, but endure it anyway, or (3) not go to that particular Sunday school.

Many churches have used this plan very effectively. Again let us emphasize that one church may find it advisable to use the auditorium adult class, whereas another church equally as spiritual may decide that it is best for them to departmentalize. Let every church be fully persuaded in its own mind. Just as the same style dress should not be placed on every woman, nor the same suit on every man, likewise the autonomy of the local church should give each church the right to follow her own leadership without coercion or criticism from outside leadership.

3. *The Single, Adult Department Plan*

This plan is a combination of the two already mentioned. For the opening assembly time all of the adults meet together. This allows for some of the advantages of suggestion 1 — the auditorium adult class. At the opening assembly special music is presented and a brief program is offered. After about a twenty-minute assembly the department divides into small classes where usually the men and women are divided. When this plan is used, the classes normally are a bit larger than when plan 2 is used. When I was pastor of the Miller Road Baptist Church in Garland, Texas, we had one large adult department with 22 classes. Eleven of these classes were for men; eleven of these classes were for ladies. (We also had one couples' class.) Each of these 22 classes would have from 20 to 60 enrolled.

This plan, too, has its advantages and disadvantages. It offers the bigness of plan 1 and the intimacy of plan 2. It offers the utilization of more workers than does plan 1, and needs less workers than plan 2. It eliminates the need of many assembly rooms as did plan 1, but it does call for much more space than plan 1 since many classrooms must be provided for the adults.

4. *The Class Plan*

This provides a number of different classes with little or no age consideration. This provides a choice for each adult. There are several couples' classes — some large and some small. There may even be several men's classes — some large and some small. A man can choose a men's class which is small or a men's class which is large. He can choose to attend a couples' class which is small or one which is large, or he may even choose a class taught in the auditorium by the pastor. A lady, likewise, can choose a ladies' class — large or small — or a couples' class — large or small — or the auditorium class.

Where there is no definite age grade in such a plan, there does, however, tend to be a gathering together of people in the same age bracket. In my present pastorate, for example, we have a young married ladies' class. Most of these ladies are in their twenties or early thirties, and in most cases their husbands do not attend Sunday school. However, some ladies older than forty find this class to their liking and attend it. This class would have perhaps sixty enrolled. There is also a small class for adult ladies with about twenty-five enrolled and has an average attendance of less than fifteen. In general, these ladies would be middle-aged or younger, though a lady of any age would be welcome. We then have a large class for middle-aged ladies. Perhaps seventy-five or eighty are enrolled in this class. Though nearly all of them are in their middle ages, it is not surprising to see both young and elderly ladies joining this class. Then we have an elderly ladies' class with about twenty-five enrolled.

This means that a lady coming to the First Baptist Church Sunday School would normally migrate with the class near her age. She would, however, have the choice of any of the aforementioned classes. Her choice might depend upon the class where her friends attend. She might want to go to a class with her mother or daughter, or she might just like a particular teacher better than the others. It might be that her husband attends Sunday school and they would like to go to a couples' class. If they so desired, they could attend our young-married couples' class, which is basically attended by couples thirty-five and under, but which welcomes couples of all ages. On the other hand, the couple might prefer to go to our New Life Class, which is basically a class for middle-aged people, though some young couples do attend. There is still another choice — the Pastor's Class in the auditorium, where several hundred people attend. Hence, a lady whose husband attends with her could choose one of seven classes, whereas a man could choose either the men's class or any one of the couple's classes.

Furthermore there are many individuals who attend the couples' classes alone. This is certainly not discouraged.

On the adult level there is never a promotion day. The young couples' class will some day become the older couples' class. The young ladies' class will some day be the older ladies' class, etc. This means that we are constantly trying to find new ideas for new classes.

There are several advantages to such a plan. As aforementioned there is a choice of classes and teachers. There is a choice concerning the size of class one would want to attend. There is also a choice as to whether to be taught by a layman or the pastor. Since we have only about a dozen adult classes, we are able to utilize our qualified teachers of adults and yet do not find it necessary to use people not especially trained to teach adults.   Then, too, hundreds of thousands of dollars have been saved by having hundreds of people meet in the auditorium. A Sunday school building to house the pastor's present class into departments and classes would cost a half million dollars in the Hammond area.

This plan also incorporates many of the ideas in plans 1, 2, and 3.   It has the auditorium class- of plan 1, but it has some classes as small as those in plan 2.   It utilizes a desirable, yet not excessive, number of teachers as does plan 3.

This eliminates completely the departmental system. There is no adult department. Neither is there an assembly of all the adults. The adults go directly to their individual classes where they have their music, announcements, and lesson. The only unit is the class, and each class is directly answerable and responsible to the Sunday school superintendent or pastor or both.

Following are the names and descriptions of the present adult classes of First Baptist Church of Hammond:

        Men's Bible Class
        Friendship Class (young married ladies)
        Bethany Class (married ladies)
        Fidelis Class (middle-aged ladies)
        Faithful Workers' Class (elderly ladies)
        Pastor's Class (for anyone)
        New Life Class (for married couples)
        Young Couples' Class
        Unmarried Adults' Class
        Spanish Class (for those who cannot under-
            stand English)
        Deaf Class
        Pioneer Class (for unmarried college-age adults)

4. Buildings and Equipment

Most growing Sunday schools find space a real problem. Having proper space is not necessary for building a large Sunday school, but it is certainly helpful. No pastor or Sunday school superintendent should use as his excuse for failure to grow the fact that the buildings are not large enough. Some of the fastest growing Sunday schools in the world have limited facilities for classrooms and departments. Realizing this we enter into a discussion of preparing physical plants for the Sunday school.

1. *Equipment.* Someone has said that one's environment is a silent, forceful teacher and that the place where people meet on the Lord's Day to study His Word and to worship has much to do with the effectiveness of what the workers are trying to do. This is certainly true! A list of essential equipment follows:

(1) There should be enough chairs to provide comfortable seating. Much care should be taken in the choosing of these chairs, and if possible, they should be well spaced allowing ample room for each pupil.

(2) Each class needs a substantial table about 28 inches high and 30 inches wide. This table should be between 40 inches and 50 inches long.

(3) Whenever it is possible to have separate rooms, curtains should be on the windows. Where it is not possible to have separate rooms, the classrooms may be divided by curtains.

(4) Each class should have a chalkboard with ample chalk and eraser.

(5) *Miscellaneous items.* It is good for classes and

departments to have songbooks, record material, maps, pictures, vases, etc. It is also very important that hooks for coats and caps be provided somewhere in the back of the room. It is also wise to have a well-tuned piano, pulpits for each teacher, good songbooks, one or two appropriate pictures, a pencil sharpener, etc. Soft, pastel colors should be used for walls and ceilings. It is wise, if at all possible, to have the front wall either darker than the other walls or be covered with a different material. Contrasting woodwork is good.

In other words, since the teaching of the Word of God is the most important thing in all the world, the best equipment possible should be provided for the Sunday school.

Of course, you may not have everything you want. In such a case, just do the best you can with what you have. The person who will not do his best under difficult conditions will also not do his best under ideal conditions. Luke 12:48 says: "...*For unto whomsoever much is given, of him shall be much required....*"

2. *Building.* Much attention is given to the church building program and the planning of the same in the author's book, *The Hyles Church Manual,* published by the Sword of the Lord, price $6.50. The following are some suggested floor plans for Sunday school departments:

(Illustration on next page)

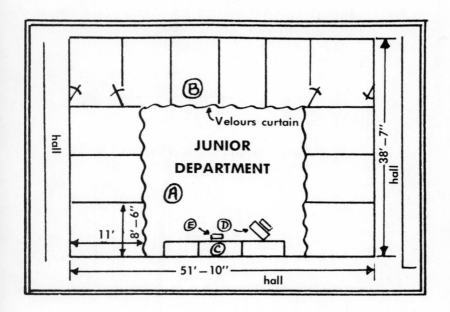

A. Assembly room
B. Classrooms
C. Closets
D. Piano
E. Speaker stand

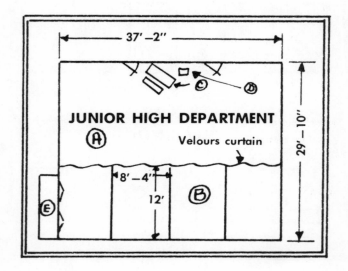

A. Assembly room
B. Classrooms
C. Piano
D. Speaker stand
E. Storage

A. **Assembly room**
B. **Classrooms**
C. **Rest rooms**
D. **Storage**
E. **Speaker stand**
F. **Piano**

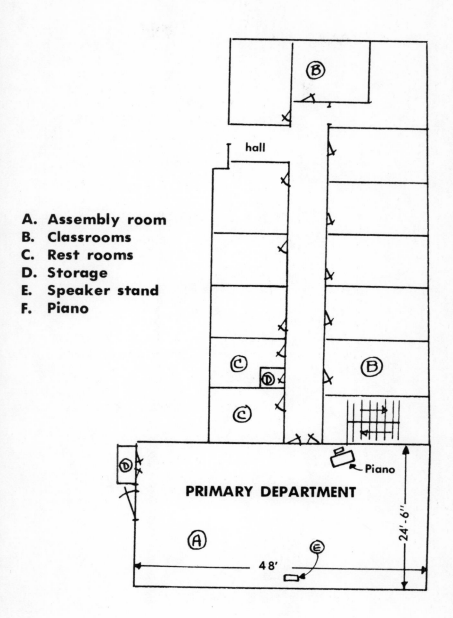

5. Publicizing the Sunday School

For too long the church has been satisfied with hiding herself in the corner and letting other institutions take the lead in publicity and advertising. Without entering into anything that is questionable, the church should certainly let its community know of its existence. In other words, the church should be kept in front of all the people all the time. There are two reasons for this: One is immediate and the other is long range. Certainly we should be working and advertising in order to reach people immediately. But on the other hand, we should always let the community be aware of the church's presence. Every time a person sees a Pepsi Cola sign, he does not immediately stop and buy a Pepsi Cola, but if the Pepsi Cola Company can implant their product in his subconscious mind, he will reach for a Pepsi Cola when he desires a soft drink. A local church should be kept so much in front of the people that when one decides to go to church, the first one he will think about is yours and mine. When Easter Sunday comes, his first attention will be toward the church that has been before him the most during the year. It is vitally important that the church publicize herself and establish an awareness on the part of the people of her existence. There are many different forms of publicity that will aid in reaching more people for the Lord Jesus Christ.

1. *Talk.* The greatest publicity in the world is the tongue. We should certainly take advantage of it. More and more the commercial people are taking advantage of the testimony. "I used a certain brand of deodorant and I finally got married." "Listerine got my man." "When I started using a

certain mouthwash, I got a raise in pay." "Folks finally started speaking to me when I used this particular soap." I use a certain washing powder and my clothes are the whitest." "I can't believe this is a non-caffeine coffee." These are statements that each of us hears regularly. The secular world has come to realize there is nothing that sells a product quite like the testimony of a satisfied customer. This is also true concerning the church. Enough people talking favorably about the church and her work can sway an entire community's attitude toward the church. Many times after a wonderful Sunday I will ask my people how many will promise to tell at least five people what God did for us on that day. If a thousand people tell five people each, five thousand people have been influenced simply by the use of the tongue. There is also no doubt that these five will continue to spread the good word until the entire area will know that something is happening at the church. Nothing will take the place of this type of publicity. The church's advocates should be busy spreading good news as the church's opponents are spreading bad news.

2. *Printed matter.* The Sunday school should take advantage of advertising through the printed page. Of course, much care should be taken to see to it that everything that goes out from the church is done properly. A particular staff member or even layman can train to be an expert on proofreading. In the First Baptist Church in Hammond a staff member has been chosen for such a task. It is her job to proofread everything that goes out of the offices. Sentence structure, proper grammar, punctuation, etc., are all checked very carefully, and every attempt is made to see to it that perfection describes the printed matter that goes out from the offices.

Another staff member has been designated as the expert on preparing brochures and other printed matter. One need not be an expert to be appointed to this task. If he has character, he will develop the knowledge and talent necessary. The pastor could tell this staff member or layman what he has in mind. This specialist then draws up a suggestion and sends it back to the pastor for approval. It may be altered, or it may be accepted as is. In some cases it may be completely vetoed, and the specialist draws up another idea.

There are several types of such publicity that may be used.

> (1) *Brochure.* This brochure is given to each person who moves to our city and to each prospect that we visit.

(2) *Promotional letter.*

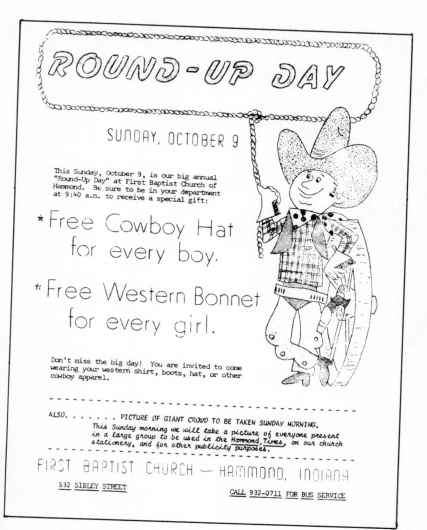

MAY 9

DEAR NURSERY PARENTS:

For the next two months your child will be hearing stories from the Bible on creation.

The month of May will be devoted to the creation of animals and birds. We feel Sunday, May 9, will be an especially good day. The children are going to see four-week old kittens. We feel the children will enjoy touching the kittens' soft fur and will enjoy watching them play.

Also on that day (May 9) each child present will receive a special gift to give Mommy for Mothers' Day.

We miss your child when he is not in Sunday School. Your child misses learning something about Jesus every Sunday he is absent.

We pray you will make a special effort to bring your child to Sunday School every week--beginning this Sunday, May 9.

Sincerely,

Mrs. Dot Barr

Nursery Department Superintendent
For the Nursery Department teachers

FIRST BAPTIST CHURCH   523 SIBLEY STREET   HAMMOND, INDIANA

JULY 31 - Big Day For JUNIOR Hi'ers

Contest . . . Between Harmond students and Outlying Area Students. Results will be based on visitors. A gift will be given to the person bringing the most visitors.

Who will win?? !!

Special Guest Speaker

Special Guests . . . Including the "Beverly Hill Billies!"

Treats For All

- -

FIRST BAPTIST CHURCH   523 SIBLEY STREET   HAMMOND, INDIANA

Jr. Hi I -- For Seventh Graders -- Ground Floor, Educational Bldg. -- Mrs. Ruskowski

Jr. Hi II -- For Eighth Graders -- Room 200, Educational Bldg. -- Mrs. Smith

Sunday School -- 9:40 a.m.

Call 932-0711 for a Bus Ride

FIRST BAPTIST CHURCH
Hammond, Indiana

CRADLE ROLL DEPARTMENT

My, How we're GROWING

Yes, we are growing by *LEAPS* and *BOUNDS* -- But nevertheless, we want to give the best care possible to your child (or children!) May we have your help:

1. If your child is not trained, bring a sufficient supply of diapers or training pants.

2. Include a plastic bag to hold wet diapers.

3. Use plastic bottles only for the nursery, unless absolutely necessary.

4. Mark bottles with the child's name. You may use the enclosed gummed labels for this. They will adhere more permanently if the bottle surface is warm and dry when they are applied.

5. Mark diaper bag with the child's name. The enclosed tag is perfect to use. If you use a plastic bag or paper sack for diapers, you can attach the tag with cellophane tape to the sack.

Take a few minutes out now to check over this list and provide for your child's identification and care in the nursery. You can help immensely by following these points.

Such letters are mailed out by departments and classes from week to week. They should be striking, attention-getting, and well-prepared. After letters have been mailed out for a period of years, some people just put them aside and do not open them. In such a case, it might be wise to put some publicity on the envelope, thereby causing the reader to have enough curiosity to open the letter. Such an envelope is shown below.

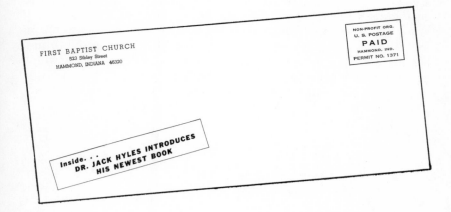

3. *Newspaper.* In some areas this is the most effective form of advertising. This is especially true in average-size cities. The city of Hammond has a population of a little over 100,000. There are perhaps another 150,000 people who live close enough to be considered prospective attenders to our services. Most of these families take the Hammond newspaper. Hence, an ad in a paper in such an area is of vital importance.

Much care should be taken to make the ad attractive and acceptable. It is usually best to steer away from anything spectacular and sensational such as announcing unheard-of sermon titles, etc. It is also wise never to use the ad as a means of attack, satire, ridicule, or slander. It should simply be used to inform the people what is going on at the church.

Such an ad may be used to advertise the sermon topics of the Lord's Day. Much care should be made by the pastor that his sermon fulfills the title. A crowd may be attracted one time by a sensational sermon title, but if the sermon is not as sensational as the title, the people will not return.

In many cities there is a Saturday church page. Some have a Friday church page. The use of this page is very important in the ministry of an evangelistic church. If possible, the fundamental church should have the largest ad on the page. If this is not possible, it should at any rate have the best prepared ad on the page. People should come to associate our churches with efficiency and properness. They may not agree with us in doctrine, convictions, or separation, but they should certainly get the idea that we know where we are going and what we are doing.

In a newspaper ad there should be one thing that stands out above everything else. Notice the following:

RIGHT

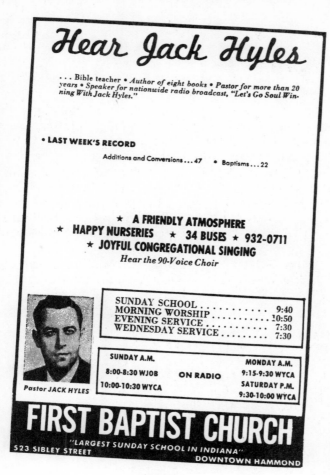

WRONG

You will notice above that one ad has nothing which stands out, but the other has something which would immediately draw one's attention as he scans the page of the paper.

The big headline of the ad should tell the story and should present the drawing card. So many churches use the word "revival." Lost sinners are not looking for revivals. The headline should be something that catches the attention of the common man.

RIGHT

WRONG

Notice above that the right ad would appeal to most any-one. The other one would appeal only to those who are already in love with Christ and His work.

The headline should usually be in thick, bold letters. Small letters may be more eyecatching than larger ones if the print is thicker. Bear in mind that the heavier the black, the more outstanding the white.

YOU ARE WANTED!
In Our Sunday School

at FIRST BAPTIST CHURCH

Every visitor is an honored guest. Thousands visit each year, from many states of our country. Make next Sunday your day to visit.

JACK HYLES
Pastor

9:40 A.M.

* A Class for Every Age
* Only the Bible Is Studied
* Qualified Bible Teachers
* Happy Nurseries

34 BUSES
932-0711

SERVICES
Sunday School 9:40

Morning Service . . 10:50

Evening Service . . . 7:30

Wednesday Service . . 7:30

LOCAL RADIO LOG
Sunday . WJOB . 8:00-8:30 A.M. — Sunday . 10:00-10:30 A.M. . WYCA
Monday-Friday . 9:15-9:30 A.M. — Saturday . 9:30-10:00 P.M. . WYCA

FIRST BAPTIST CHURCH
"LARGEST SUNDAY SCHOOL IN INDIANA"
523 SIBLEY STREET   DOWNTOWN HAMMOND

WRONG

MORE PARKING

The first FIRST BAPTIST CHURCH BUILDING RAZED

—to give way to the growth and progress of the church. More parking will be available on this site for those attending the church services.

520 Sibley Street— Across From Main Auditorium

The building pictured here was built in 1910 and was used as the main auditorium until 1913. It was sold in 1913 and repurchased in 1964 after the large fire that destroyed two buildings owned by First Baptist Church.

Sunday School . . . . 9:40 A.M.
Morning Service . . . . 10:50 A.M.
Evening Service . . . . 7:00 P.M.
Wednesday Service . . . . 7:30 P.M.

LOCAL RADIO SCHEDULE
Monday-Friday • WYCA • 9:00 A.M.
Saturday • WYCA • 9:00 A.M.
Sunday • WJOB • 8:00 A.M.

FIRST BAPTIST CHURCH
"Largest Sunday School in Indiana"

523 SIBLEY STREET

DOWNTOWN HAMMOND

RIGHT

Notice that the wrong ad has big lettering but is skinny and does not stand out from the ad, whereas the bolder, blacker print catches one's eye immediately.

It is best to have a church ad near the margin of the paper. It is even better to have it placed in the corner.

Appropriate pictures should be used regularly for the church ads. Especially is it good to use pictures that are unique and that tell the story of the church and Sunday school. Pictures of people should be used more sparingly. Following you will see several ads that do and some that do not use pictures to their best advantage.

RIGHT

RIGHT

WRONG

WRONG

WRONG

You will notice above that we have used pictures of progress and pictures that tell the story of the First Baptist Church. These are also pictures that deal with the uniqueness of the church. This is a very important feature in advertising. One of our mottos is, "The difference is worth the distance." Therefore, it is wise to be reminding the people constantly of what the differences are. This should not, of course, be used to point out the weaknesses of sister churches, but rather the strengths of ours.

Of course, such advertising is expensive. There are several ways that such expenses can be raised.

(1) *The budget.* This is, of course, the best way. Several hundred dollars, or several thousand dollars could be designated from the budget for publicity purposes. This is the painless and easy way.

(2) *The Wednesday night offering.* Many churches do not have an offering on Wednesday night. Such an offering can be taken and used for special purposes over and above the regular budget. This one could be used for advertising. In past times it has been suggested that people give all of the change in their pockets, and this money can be used for publicity.

(3) *Departments and classes.* Each adult class could be responsible for an ad periodically. Suppose the Sunday school has ten classes and ten departments, then each group would be responsible for the newspaper advertising one week out of twenty.

Advertising pays off. It does not immediately pay for itself, but in the end it will more than do so.

Some Sunday schools and churches will be unable to afford big ads. This, of course, can be compensated by attractiveness and proper content. Below are some sample small advertisements.

50 VOICE CHOIR

This Sunday night, in connection with the regular preaching service, our Choir will present a Christmas Cantata. The Service Begins at 7:00 P.M. and YOU Are Invited To Come.

Merry Christmas

The Staff and Membership of our Church join hands in wishing a very "Merry Christmas" to all our Calumet Region Friends.

523 . SIBLEY . ST.

Hammond

SUNDAY SCHOOL ... 9:40 A.M.
MORNING SERVICE 10:50 A.M.
EVENING SERVICE ...7:00 P.M.

LAST WEEK'S RECORD
Sunday School Attendance 1012
CONVERSIONS and Additions... 31
BAPTISMS 5

For Transportation to Sunday School and Church ... Call WE 2-8711

FIRST BAPTIST CHURCH

As the church begins to grow and as the income increases, more and more should be designated for advertising. As the ads become larger and larger they will be along the lines of those below:

HEART TRANSPLANTS

in the Light of the Scriptures

JACK HYLES

Hear this timely sermon by Pastor Hyles

SUNDAY
JAN. 21—7:00 P.M.
EVENING

These questions will be discussed:

Does the Bible speak about heart transplants?

Is it morally wrong? Is man playing God?

Is it Scriptural to prolong life?

Does a new heart change a person's personality or character?

Sunday School .... 9:40 A.M.	**LOCAL RADIO SCHEDULE**
Morning Service .... 10:50 A.M.	Monday-Friday • WYCA • 9:00 A.M.
Evening Service .... 7:00 P.M.	Saturday • WYCA • 9:00 A.M.
Wednesday Service .... 7:30 P.M.	Sunday • WJOB • 8:00 A.M.

FIRST BAPTIST CHURCH
"Largest Sunday School in Indiana"

523 SIBLEY STREET   DOWNTOWN HAMMOND

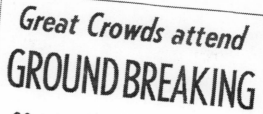

Great Crowds attend
GROUND BREAKING
New Education Building

PASTOR HYLES READS messages of commendation from many friends, and interested persons . . . many from congressmen, senators, governors, from J. Edgar Hoover and a letter from **THE WHITE HOUSE.**

GROUND-BREAKING 1966

Below, crowd faces speakers stand and site of ½ million dollar education building to be constructed.

LAST SUNDAY'S RECORD
• Sunday School ...... 2,837 • Baptisms 23
• Additions and Conversions 61 • Buses 1,067
34 Bus Routes

	LOCAL RADIO LOG	
MON. FRI. • WYCA • 9:15-9:30 A.M.		
SATURDAY • WYCA • 9:30 P.M.		SUN. • WJOB • 8:00 A.M.
		SUN. • WYCA • 10:00 A.M.

FIRST BAPTIST CHURCH
"LARGEST SUNDAY SCHOOL IN INDIANA"
523 SIBLEY STREET   DOWNTOWN HAMMOND

64 THE HYLES SUNDAY SCHOOL MANUAL

When churches become large and budgets become big, there are times when full-page ads or half-page ads are desirable. Several times in my ministry we have used even a small section of the paper for the church. Some sample larger ads are seen below:

Follow the crowd to...

FILL THE CIVIC CENTER FOR CHRIST

Monday-March 18th-7:00 P.M.

Pastor Jack Hyles

Opening the ↘

5th Annual Nationwide
PASTORS' SCHOOL
First Baptist Church • 523 Sibley St., Hammond

and the

National
SWORD of the LORD CONVENTION
↓

Musical Guests
LAKE CENTRAL HIGH SCHOOL BAND
Hear the
250 VOICE CHOIR
Special guests include:

★ Lt. Governor Rock, Area Mayors, Legislators, and Out of Town Visitors
★ Hundreds of Ministers from across America

Hammond Civic Center
5825 SOHL AVENUE   HAMMOND

Friday, April 10, 1964   THE HAMMOND TIMES   ★ Page C-7

MAY WE SHOW YOU OUR
NEW AUDITORIUM

2374 ATTENDED
LAST SUNDAY

The 2,200 seat auditorium as seen from the choir

The lower floor as seen from the main entrance

With Gratitude
To God
We Take You
Inside Our
New Building

The vestibule (entirely carpeted) as seen from the entrance

The support for balcony as seen by the eye of the architect

JOIN US IN THESE SERVICES
SUNDAY

9:45 A.M. .... SUNDAY SCHOOL
10:45 A.M. .... MORNING SERVICE
7:00 P.M. .... EVENING SERVICE

8:00 A.M. .... RADIO SERVICE—WJOB
10:00 A.M. ...... RADIO BIBLE CLASS—WYCA-FM
9:30 P.M. .... RADIO SERVICE—WYCA-FM

The 67-Voice Choir leads in singing praises to God

Hundreds of people attended the 3:00 p.m. Dedication Service

FIRST BAPTIST CHURCH
523 SIBLEY STREET   HAMMOND, IND.
Jack Hyles, Pastor

The local church should also take advantage of news releases.   The newspaper should be flooded with interesting articles about the church.   These should usually be accompanied by pictures.   Such things could be written up in articles: "The Adopting of the Church Budget," "The Adopting of Plans for a New Building," "Ground-breaking Day," "Promotion Day," "Dedication Day," and other special days along with articles about special guests who appear from time to time at the church.   Following are some sample articles:

Pastors Study

State Sen. Eugene Bainbridge (D., Munster); Dr. John R. Rice, editor of a Christian publication; Dr. Jack Hyles of First Baptist Church and Mayor Richard Collins of Crown Point check the program at opening session of the annual Pastors' School in the Hammond Civic Center.

6,000 Attend School

HAMMOND — The fifth annual national Pastors' School opened Monday night with leaders in religion, business and government among the estimated 6,000 at the first session in the Civic Center.

Lt. Gov. Robert L. Rock wel comed the pastors from approximately 40 states and others to Indiana. Rock represented Gov. Roger D. Branigin.

He commended the church in general and the First Baptist Church of Hammond in particular for "work in behalf of God."

THE EVENT is sponsored by the Hammond church.

Mayor Joseph E. Klen welcomed the guests to Hammond.

"This is one of my finest days thus far in my administration," he said.

Dr. Jack Hyles, pastor of First Baptist Church, said "perhaps we cannot win America but we can win enough to Christ to stay God's hand of judgment on this nation."

He said:

"IT IS TIME Christians became angered at such things as LSD, loose morals and dirty literature. Every voice who believes in Gold should be raised against such things."

Other sessions of the school will be during the week in the First Baptist Church, 523 Sibley St.

Its purpose is to teach pastors methods of increasing attendance and improving the efficiency of the work in their churches.

Classes include instruction in visitation, finances, music, promotion, Sunday School, administration, rescue mission work,

work with the deaf, church secretarial work and nurseries.

A MEETING of the staff of "The Sword of The Lord," a weekly publication edited by Dr. John R. Rice in Murfreesboro, Tenn., will be a part of the program.

Dr. Rice was introduced Monday. He is author of several books on religion.

Among the demonstrations during the school will be a wedding and a funeral service. Pastors will be shown the proper procedures to follow.

A choir of more than 200 voices sang "America" during Monday's opening session.

The Lake Central High School Band of St. John played selections.

Baptists Buy Original Building

THE ORIGINAL First Baptist Church building is a Hammond landmark.

As is the case in all advertising through printed matter, the articles should also be done properly, attractively, and neatly. Nothing but the best should represent the Lord's work.

The pastor should never become offended if his articles are not used. A good relationship should be developed between the church and the news media. Patience and kindness should characterize all of our relationships with the outside world. The news media should know the church and the pastor as the friendliest and most courteous institution and person in town. Occasionally a note of gratitude should be written from the church to responsible authorities of the newspaper and to others who help in the advertising program.

4. *The radio.* The use of the radio, like the use of the newspaper, will vary in its effectiveness in certain areas. We have a varied radio ministry. At the time of this writing we have a nationwide broadcast presented on approximately fifty stations across America and the Caribbean. This, of course, is a needed ministry, but it does not immediately affect the ministry of the local church. What does affect the ministry of the local church, however, is our daily radio broadcast called "The Pastor's Study," which is heard locally from 9:00 to 9:30 each weekday morning. In some areas the population listens to the local radio station, but in other areas it is almost completely overlooked. If used properly the local station can be a great help to the church. Following are some suggestions regarding the local broadcast:

(1) *It is not usually a good evangelistic ministry.* Most of the people who hear religious broadcasts are already Christian people who have a desire to hear the Word preached. Very few unsaved people voluntarily hear a gospel broadcast. The fact is, however, that some do, and enough Gospel should be presented to reach them.

(2) *A daily broadcast is usually best.* Someone has said that a weekly broadcast promotes the church and that a daily broadcast promotes the preacher. This may or may not be true, but it certainly is true that a daily broadcast can promote both, and it is necessary to do both. It is necessary to do both in order to get people to come to the church to hear the preacher. It is certainly not pride nor sin for a church to attempt to get people to come to hear the pastor. This, of course, must be done within bounds and should not include bragging, boasting, etc. A daily broadcast, if done properly, can be used to acquaint the community with the activities and work of the church so as to arouse curiosity and desire in the hearts of those in the area.

(3) *A daily broadcast should include intriguing announcements about the church activities.* This is one of the main purposes for a daily broadcast.

On Monday morning, for example, we like to read the reports of the previous day. Naturally we stress the good things that happened. We try to whet the appetites of the listeners so that they will have a desire to attend our services. Throughout the week we keep before the people the activities of the coming Sunday, or for that matter, all of the activities of the week. As the week nears its end we stress more heavily the wonderful things to which we are looking on the next Sunday.

(4) *The pastor should be a friend of the listener.* A personal feeling should exist between the pastor and the radio listener. In a real sense the radio listener should feel that he has a radio pastor. We do some preaching on our daily broadcast, but for the most part it is a folksy, neighborly chat with the people of our area. This is a great help in improving the church's image as well as the preacher's image in the community. Many times people get the idea that the fundamental church is hard-boiled, and that the preacher trips old ladies as they walk across the street and pushes little children in front of cars. This fallacy can be refuted by a kind, passionate, tender voice coming daily from the church to the community.

(5) *Good, well-planned music should be used.* From one-third to one-half of the broadcast perhaps should be good gospel music. Well-trained voices should be used and well-rehearsed specials should be presented. It seems unwise to stereotype one's church in the minds of the community by using anything but good, solid, tested gospel numbers. We have found that the people are blessed and the church is helped by the use of such numbers as "The Old Rugged Cross," "Rock of Ages," "At Calvary," and the songs that have been tested through the years. We stay away from novelty numbers except as an occasional exception. It should definitely be established in the minds of the hearers that the church uses good music and prepares it well.

More and more of the secular stations are turning to musical programs. The church could certainly learn a lesson from this and present good, solid, musical numbers on the broadcast.

(6) *The name of the broadcast.* The naming of the broadcast should come after its format is planned. When the format is established, the broadcast's name should be descriptive of the format. Since our broadcast comes from the pastor's study, and is conducted by the pastor as he sits at his desk, we call it simply, "The Pastor's Study." We attempt to make the listener feel that he is in the study listening to the pastor. It is a chatty, "howdy-neighbor" kind of a get-together. The name should not be trite or overly used and should be chosen with prayer and care.

(7) *The theme.* The theme song of the broadcast should be one that helps to tell what is to come. For example, on the Pastor's Study broadcast, it would be unwise to begin with the singing of the "Battle Hymn of the Republic." However, on a broadcast originating in the auditorium of the church, when the entire church service is presented, one would not want to start the broadcast with the theme song, "Turn Your Eyes Upon Jesus." The theme song should be appropriate and descriptive. It should be a forerunner of what is to come.

(8) *A typical daily broadcast.*
   a. *The theme.*
   b. *Introduction and words of welcome by the pastor.*
   c. *Some special musical number.* The pastor should gradually introduce the number. A few words can be said about the song. We avoid such trite statements as, "Here is a beautiful little number," "Now God bless Mrs. Jones as she comes to sing for us," etc. Suppose the number is "Does Jesus Care?" The pastor may simply lead into it by saying something like this: "Many of our listeners have burdens and heartaches today. Many times in the midst of

burdens and heartaches we wonder if anybody really cares. The world is so busy and people are in such a hurry that so few have time to care and so few who have the time have the heart to do so. We can be thankful to God that there is One who cares. The ladies' trio now comes to tell you who He is." Immediately the song is sung. Such is the case of all of the special musical numbers that follow.

In some cases the music will be broadcast live. We find it necessary, however, to tape scores of numbers and professionally play them on our daily broadcast. The pastor's portion is live, but the numbers are played by tape. Proper planning with the radio station in the purchase of proper equipment will make the broadcast seem live. There are multitudes of people who think the singers are actually in the pastor's study each morning.

d. *A thought for the day.* We keep several files of thoughts. From various religious periodicals we clip points, provocative thoughts, etc., and use one each morning. We prefer something that is striking and thought-provoking. It may be something that is comforting. It may be something concerning a current event that is alarming. It is always something to stir the minds of the listeners.

e. *The chuckle for the day.* Here is something that we have recently started on our broadcast. This is not a telling of a joke, as such, but some little humorous incident that can be told in fifteen to thirty seconds. Usually it is about a preacher or a church. A few days ago I told a little story about a man who brought his dog to church. The preacher made the dog leave. After the service the man gave the preacher $25.00. The preacher could not understand why he had done so, especially since he insisted that the dog leave. He asked the man, "Why did you give me $25.00 after I had made you take your dog out of the services?"

The man replied, "Pastor, it was certainly worth $25.00 for my dog not to have to listen to that sermon."

Of course, the chuckle should be brief and refreshing or else it would not be wise to have it at all.

f. *The second special song.*

g. *Happy birthday time.*   It was Pastor Tom Wallace from Elkton, Maryland, that introduced me to this idea.   He had used it with great delight.   We simply get the birthdays of all of the people we can and call their names on their birthday.   The staff comes into the pastor's study to sing "Happy Birthday" to them. Many look forward to this part of the broadcast each day.

h. *"It happened on your birthday."*   We try to find interesting things in Christian history as well as secular history that happened on each day of the year. This way we can interest those having birthdays by telling what other famous event took place on their birthday.

i. *Third special number.* This number is dedicated to those having birthdays.

j. *The prayer list.*   At the first of each broadcast the pastor says a word about those who have need of prayer. He encourages them to call the church office and tell the people of their prayer needs.   It is nothing unusual to have sixty or seventy people to call in during the course of the broadcast.   The secretaries take the prayer requests, bring them to the pastor, and at prayer-list time, he reads each name and each request for prayer.   Then he prays for each person by name and by request.   This normally takes about seven to eight minutes. This is a wonderful way to be of service to those who have need of prayer.

k. *Fourth and last special number.* This can be dedicated to those who called in for prayer.

This number perhaps could be one that is comforting, such as "What a Friend We Have in Jesus," "Rock of Ages," etc.

1. *Message.* From five to fifteen minutes may be left for the message if the aforementioned things have been expedited properly. Sometimes the pastor gives the message earlier in the broadcast and then ends with prayer time. This message may come anywhere. For that matter he may get a thought from the reading of "It happened on your birthday," and he may take five or ten minutes then. Perhaps he may have his mind provoked by the "thought for the day" and take awhile to discuss this and bring his message at that time. In most cases, however, the pastor would want to close the broadcast with his message.

There are other ways in which the church could use the radio. A weekly broadcast may be of benefit. In such a case it should not be as folksy as the one above. It should be a little bigger and a little more impressive.

Some churches use spot announcements to good advantage. This is certainly worth consideration.

For many years I broadcasted my Sunday school class live over a local station. Some churches like to broadcast their services. At any rate, or whatever the type broadcast, the Sunday school should be stressed over and over again. Probably more people attend the church during the Sunday school hour than during any other hour of the week. This makes it an important time. Certainly the Sunday school should receive the bulk of the advertising on radio. Goals, attendances, drives, pushes, special days, etc., should be kept before the people on every radio broadcast.

Again let us emphasize the importance of doing God's work properly. The pastor and musicians should take care in the planning of the broadcast. It should be interesting to all and offensive to none as far as presentation is concerned. We may offend people by our convictions but let us not be offensive by doing God's work in a lackadaisical way. It is the most important work in the world; let us treat it as such.

5. *Church Signs.* The first impression that many people get of a local church is from signs. Because of that, much care and preparation should be taken in the choosing and purchasing of church signs.

(1) *The sign should be proportionate in size with the church plant.* The church with a large physical plant should have a sign proportionately large. A church with a small plant should, of course, have a sign in ratio with the size of the building.

(2) *The sign should be professionally planned and made.* Literally thousands of church signs need painting and even editing. It is unbelievable that some churches even misspell the name of their church. I have seen Baptist spelled "Babtist" and "Babptist." In other cases, the sign is so old or so poorly done that people cannot read the printing. In some other cases the church does not even have a sign. This is completely unbelievable and yet true.

(3) *Sensationalism, deceit, and provocation should be omitted on the church sign.* The sign is not to preach a sermon. It is simply to identify the church. Many signs are so provocative that they prevent people from coming to the services. The church can state her position in such short, terse language on a sign so as to keep people from hearing that position as preached in power and energy of the Holy Spirit from the pulpit. How tragic!

It is also wise for the sign to be very honest in its content. A church could be the fastest-growing church in town and words to that effect could be placed on the sign (though I doubt the wisdom of this). The next year, however, the church may not grow as rapidly. The sign could become dishonest. The church should always be honest with the public and never in the least deceitful. The product should always contain the contents listed on the cover. This is especially true in the Lord's work.

(4) *There are many different types of signs that can be utilized in the life of a church:*

a. *The changeable copy panel.*
A nice, conservative changeable sign used to advertise the current work, activities, and ministry of the church can oftentimes be of benefit. Much care should be taken that this sign does not look like a theatre marquee. Hence, it probably should not be located over the main entrance, and it should be much more conservative than a theatre-type **marquee.** A flat, solid, changeable copy panel is preferable for a church. Some churches find it beneficial to have the main permanent sign and changeable sign in one unit. Regardless of the size, shape, and location of the changeable sign, it should be used only for advertisement, inspiration, etc. It could announce the coming of special speakers or the title of Sunday's message. Again, sensationalism should usually be avoided. To say the least, sermon subjects on the sign should never be exaggerated, and the sermon contents should certainly be up to the announced sermon subject.

The following are some advertisements that have been used on the changeable sign of the First Baptist Church of Hammond.

"Heart Transplants in the Light of Scripture" Sunday, January 12   7:00 p.m.

Helpful Lessons on Marriage   Taught by Pastor Hyles   Sundays at 9:40 a.m. & 6:00 p.m.

Unique Old-Fashioned Service   Sunday, October 23   7:00 p.m.

"Let's Go Soul Winning with Jack Hyles" WYCA 9:00 a.m. Sat.   WJOB 8:00 a.m. Sun. Heard over 40 Stations

Free Bus Service   53 Routes Covering the Calumet   Call 932-0711

Speaking Here Sunday, October 29 Dr. R. G. Lee of Memphis   10:50 a.m.   7:00 p.m.

Adult Rally with Dr. Bill Rice   Sunday, Aug. 7   9:40 a.m.

Preaching the Gospel Here Since 1887
Preaching a Literal Heaven and Hell Sunday
Services 10:50 a.m. 7:30 p.m.
Preaching Jesus Christ—the Only Way to
Heaven Sundays 10:50 - 7:00 p.m.

b. *Church buses.*

Many churches utilize buses in their transportation program. When this is done, these buses
should be attractively painted. Each bus should
become a rolling signboard. It is best to steer
away from spectacularism, but certainly some
good advertisement could be used in the publi-
cizing of the church as the buses roll through
the streets of the city. At this writing the First
Baptist Church of Hammond operates 60 bus
routes.   This gives us 60 rolling signboards
which cover the city of Hammond. Not only
do they advertise the church on Sunday, but
throughout the entire week. These buses are
not serviced at the same service stations or ga-
rages, but rather at strategic locations throughout the entire area. This means that these 60
church buses are parked all over, giving us 60
billboards. Again let me emphasize the importance of the lettering and painting being professionally done and well done.

At times it might be wise to ask someone just
to drive the buses around town. Think how
many people can see one church bus in a day's
time as it is driven up and down the streets of
the city.

c. *Miscellaneous signs.*

Some churches have utilized the advertising
space of park benches. Others have purchased
the space on sides or backs of city buses. Still
others have front license plates for the cars of
their members. (This is done only in states
which do not use state license tags on the front
as well as the back.) We have found it wise to
have the church's name neatly engraved on the
back of the custodian's uniforms. Over and

over again we are simply saying: Keep the name of the church before the people all the time. A community should always be church-conscious, and the fundamental church should take the lead in advertising.

6. *Letters.* The Sunday school should make much use of the mail. Hundreds of thousands of letters from the First Baptist Church of Hammond are sent each year. Seldom is the week when hundreds of letters are not sent through the mail. Sometimes these are churchwide mailings. In other cases they are mailed to departments or even classes. Samples of such letters follow:

ALL THIS WILL BE HAPPENING ON OCTOBER 3 AT FIRST BAPTIST CHURCH OF HAMMOND --

☆ A COWBOY HAT FOR EVERYONE

Everyone attending Sunday School October 3 will receive a paper cowboy hat saying, "First Baptist Church, Hammond, Indiana---Round-Up Day 1965."

☆ BIG PICTURE TO BE TAKEN

We will take a mass picture of everyone with their cowboy hats. Then another picture will be taken without hats for our church stationery.

☆ DR. BILL RICE TO BE HERE

Special guests for the day will be two real cowboys--Dr. Bill Rice and his son, Pete Rice, from Murfreesboro, Tennessee.

☆ SHETLAND PONY GIVEN AWAY

The boy or girl who brings the most visitors to Sunday School on October 3 will be given free a real Shetland pony.

-- SO BE SURE TO BE HERE AND WEAR YOUR COWBOY REGALIA! MANY FOLKS ARE PLANNING TO WEAR COWBOY SHIRTS, HATS, BOOTS, AND OTHER THINGS WESTERN.

SUNDAY, OCTOBER 3

First Baptist Church	Sunday School - 9:40 a.m.
523 Sibley St.	For Bus Transportation -
Hammond, Indiana	Call 932-0711

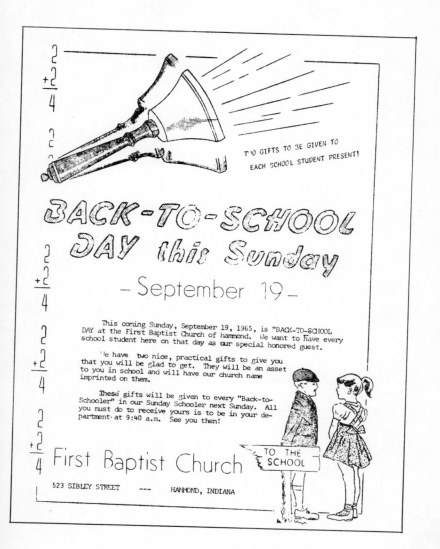

TWO GIFTS TO BE GIVEN TO EACH SCHOOL STUDENT PRESENT!

BACK-TO-SCHOOL DAY this Sunday
– September 19 –

This coming Sunday, September 19, 1965, is "BACK-TO-SCHOOL DAY at the First Baptist Church of Hammond. We want to have every school student here on that day as our special honored guest.

We have two nice, practical gifts to give you that you will be glad to get. They will be an asset to you in school and will have our church name imprinted on them.

These gifts will be given to every "Back-to-Schooler" in our Sunday Schooler next Sunday. All you must do to receive yours is to be in your department at 9:40 a.m. See you then!

First Baptist Church

523 SIBLEY STREET   ---   HAMMOND, INDIANA

TO THE SCHOOL

ALL BEGINNER CHILDREN -- Come to the Beginner Department April 24 at 9:40 a.m.

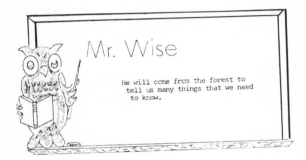

Come to a Puppet Show
Next Sunday

Mr. Wise

He will come from the forest to tell us many things that we need to know.

Silly Willy

He will come from the forest, too, to learn many things that Mr. Wise will teach him.

It will be fun, and we will learn something, too.

SUNDAY, APRIL 24 - BEGINNER DEPARTMENT - FIRST BAPTIST CHURCH OF HAMMOND, INDIANA

HOW MANY CHARMS DO YOU HAVE FOR YOUR KEY CHAIN OR BRACELET?

Come next Sunday and get another one. You'll get one every Sunday for a few more Sundays.

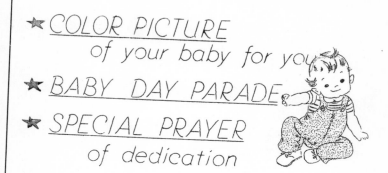

★ COLOR PICTURE
of your baby for you

★ BABY DAY PARADE

★ SPECIAL PRAYER
of dedication

Dear Parent:

Sunday, October 17, is our Annual "Baby Day" at First Baptist Church. There are several features of this day as follows:

1. Your baby's picture will be taken in color, placed in a lovely folder, and given to you as a gift and a reminder of Baby Day, 1965.

2. The preaching service Sunday morning will end several minutes earlier than usual. Before baptism, the parents will be asked to go to the nurseries and get the babies to bring back to the auditorium for a "Baby Day Parade" around the building. Dress your baby in his nicest attire, and we will show him off to the people in this parade.

3. A special prayer of dedication will be offered for all babies born since last "Baby Day."

Baby Day is for all children three and under. (That is, all children who have not yet been promoted to the Beginner Department.) Be sure and have your child here on time Sunday morning and take him to his department as usual. We will start taking pictures at 9:15 a.m. as the babies begin to arrive and will be taking them all during the Sunday School and preaching hours. We hope to see your baby Sunday. God bless you.

Sincerely,

Jack Hyles
Pastor

FIRST BAPTIST CHURCH - 523 SIBLEY STREET - HAMMOND, INDIANA - SUNDAY SCHOOL AT 9:40 AM

6. Sunday Morning Schedule

This chapter will be largely review. It shall consist of the tying together of what has previously been said about Sunday school class and its organization, work and activities on Sunday. We will start at the beginning of the day and go through the entire Sunday morning schedule.

1. *The teacher should get up early enough so as to avoid any rushing.*

2. *The teacher should brush over his lesson for the task at hand.*

3. *He should dress himself properly so as to be a good example.*

4. *He should arrive fifteen minutes early to prepare the classroom and the pupil for the lesson.* ·

5. *He should then stand at the door to greet the class members as they enter.*

6. *The teacher should properly meet and greet all visitors before the starting of the opening assembly or the class.*

7. *Perhaps the sunshine chairman has arrived by now to add some sunshine and cheer to the class.*

8. *The vice-president is at the back of the room or at the door of the room sharing with others the privilege of greeting the members and visitors as they enter.*

9. *The secretary is passing out the envelopes, membership slips, and visitor's cards.*

10. *The vice-president may be introducing the visitors to other members as they come in.* All of this together makes them feel at home.

11. *The pianist has arrived at least ten minutes early and is playing the prelude.* The prelude should be one that

moves along rapidly and one which creates a spirit of fellowship in the class.

12. *The songleader has also arrived early enough to pick out the songs and discuss them with the pianist.*

13. *At the exact starting time (not one minute later) the superintendent should call the department to order and introduce the music director who in turn leads in a well-planned congregational song.* Well-known choruses can be used. Certainly all songs should be familiar to the majority of the people.

14. *The departmental superintendent then presents a well-planned, brief opening assembly.* This opening assembly should include adequate welcoming of visitors. It may or may not tie in with the lesson, but it certainly should be something pertinent to the needs of the pupils. The entire opening exercise in the departmental assembly room should last no longer than ten minutes. For a Sunday school that lasts one hour, this gives ten minutes for time spent in going to the classes and in business.

In the opening assembly time, the superintendent should certainly promote attendance for future Sundays, give honor to those who have done good jobs in the past, and instill and inspire in the hearts of the pupils the desire to bring others with them.

15. *The teacher then stands at the door of the classroom and welcomes the pupils as they enter.* In case there is no opening assembly in the department, things aforementioned should be done such as passing out of envelopes, the vice-president welcoming the visitors, etc.

16. *The teacher or president calls the class to order.* This should, of course, be done in a winning way and should immediately be impressive to members and visitors alike.

17. *Much attention should be given to the visitors.* They may be introduced by the teacher, the president, the vice-president, or the group captain. Whoever does it should be effervescent in his welcome.

18. *Class business.* This should be limited basically to the announcements. All planning of socials and extracurricular activities should be done prior to class time, and business cared for in the class should be limited to announcements, simple promotion, etc.

19. *The teaching of the lesson.* The president introduces the teacher. The teacher puts his heart, mind, body, and soul into the teaching of the Word of God. His lesson should include a title, a point of contact, body or general teaching, a conclusion, and an appeal.

20. *The class may close with a report of the secretary and others if needed, such people as mission chairman, sunshine chairman, social chairman, etc.* As mentioned in another chapter, the reports should be limited to thirty seconds or less.

At the end of the class the members should be told about the preaching service and should be encouraged to attend.

This sums up the activities of a Sunday morning. Certainly other things could and should be added, and in some cases, some of these suggestions could be omitted. The purpose of this chapter is not necessarily to tell the Sunday school superintendent and teachers what to do, but rather to impress upon them the importance of doing well what they do. The teaching of the Word of God is the biggest thing in all the world. Let us treat is as such.

7. The Enlistment and Qualifications of Sunday School Teachers

"Then saith he unto his disciples, The harvest truly is plenteous, but the labourers are few; Pray ye therefore the Lord of the harvest, that he will send forth labourers into his harvest." —Matt. 9:37,38.

What could be more important than the teaching of the Word of God? Hence, what could be more important in the Sunday school than the proper choosing of the teachers? The enlistment of the Sunday school teacher should be done with dignity, spiritual insight, and God's leadership. It should not be taken lightly. It is tragic, but true, that the average five-and-ten-cent store gives more thought in carefully selecting a clerk than the average church does in selecting a pastor, and Sunday school teachers are often chosen almost flippantly. They are often enlisted by telephone or through a conversation in a church hallway, or casually in a public meeting place. Eastern Airlines would not choose a pilot this way. Is a pilot more important than a teacher of the Word of God? The Hilton Hotel chain would not even choose a maid that way. Is a maid more important than a teacher of the Word of God? Certainly no school board would choose a public schoolteacher that way. Is a public schoolteacher more important than a teacher of the Word of God? When will God's people realize that the biggest business in all the world is God's business and it should be treated as such?

A number of years ago one of our staff members was enlisting a Sunday school worker outside the teachers' and officers' meeting in the hallway. I overheard the conversation and immediately called this staff member to my office for a conference. I asked, "Do you think the Hammond school board chooses schoolteachers that way?"

Of course, the answer was, "No."

"If you were on the school board, would you choose teachers that way?"

Again the answer was, "No."

"Then do you think the schoolteachers are more important than Sunday school teachers?"

The answer again was, "No."

"Why then," I asked, "would you give more care in the selection of a schoolteacher than one who teaches the Word of God?"

Oh, when will God's people realize that the biggest thing in all the world is God's business — the teaching of God's Word and the carrying out of God's program?

1. *The pastor and/or the Sunday school superintendent should check the church roll regularly for prospective teachers.*

Each person on the roll should be carefully and regularly considered for a teaching position. This gives all equal opportunity and prevents the overlooking of anyone.

2. *A list of prospective teachers should be kept.*

As the roll is being checked the names of good teaching prospects should be listed. Then these people should be carefully observed and checked before being contacted about teaching.

3. *Enlisting should be done at the prospect's home or in the church office.*

This is no task to be cared for by telephone. Neither is this a little, casual job to be looked upon lightly. The visit should be highly spiritual, very serious, and in a spirit of prayer. It should be done with a dignity of a personnel office of a big corporation choosing a key man for a position. The one doing the enlisting should carefully explain to the prospective worker that he has prayed about a vacancy in the Sunday school and that he believes God has led him to that individual.

4. *The conversation should be begun with prayer.* The person doing the enlisting should do the praying, asking

for God to lead in the discussion and the decision that is soon to be made. Remember this is God's business; we need His help and leadership.

5. *The work should be presented to the prospective teacher.* He should be told that the job will not be an easy one, but a hard one. He should be challenged by the task. People respond better to a real challenge. Such statements as these should not be used: "Oh, it is easy." "Anybody could do it." "It won't take much time." Instead such statements as these should be used: "This is a very important job." "It will definitely take much of your time." "We will ask you to keep certain rules and perform certain duties." Teaching Sunday school is not a job for an inexperienced baby-sitter, rather for a diligent teacher of the Word of God. One does not have to have a seminary degree or a Bible college diploma, but he should have a definite understanding that he is expected to do a job and to do it well and that the job is both rewarding and exacting.

6. *Present the duties to the prospective teacher.*

He should be told about the size of the class, visiting of the absentees, the faithfulness to the class, the hour of the Teachers' and Officers' Meeting, the location of the classroom, etc. No stones should be left unturned in the presentation of these duties. It is better to have a good understanding before the enlistment than a misunderstanding after the enlistment.

7. *Present clearly the qualifications for teaching in the Sunday school.* They are as follows:

   (1) *Live a separated life.* No one should teach in the Sunday school who is not separate from the world. Certainly no one should be allowed to teach in the Sunday school who drinks alcoholic beverages in any form. No one should be allowed to teach in the Sunday school who uses tobacco in any form. No one should be allowed to teach in the Sunday school who frequents such places as the theatre, dances, card parties, etc. Needless to say, the things listed above do not complete the list of qualifications of separation. Perhaps each church would have her own peculiar convictions that should be included. Now these convictions should

not be simply preferences, and they should not be simply pet peeves of a few biased church members, but rather the deep-rooted convictions of the church and pastor.

(2) *Be a tither.* Malachi reminds that failing to tithe is robbing God. Jesus commends tithing, and no one should teach in the Sunday school who does not practice this Bible command.

(3) *Be faithful to the public services of the church.* It should be explained that the teachers are expected to be in the Sunday school, to attend the Sunday morning service, the Sunday evening service, and the Wednesday evening service. Those in places of leadership should set the example for those who follow. This example should certainly include faithfulness to the public services.

(4) *Be loyal to the pastor and the church program.* This does not mean that the teacher must believe everything that the pastor believes, or even agree with everything that the church does in its program. It does mean, however, that as long as there is no moral issue involved, the person will cooperate with the desires of the majority and be loyal to the pastor as he presents this program under God. Perhaps the most important qualification for "followship" is loyalty.

(5) *Be faithful to the class.* It should be explained to the prospective teacher that he would be expected to be in the class regularly. Now there will be a few Sundays in a year that a person would be on vacation, sick, or on a necessary weekend trip. However, people who have to go out of town for one weekend a month certainly should not be considered as prospective teachers.

(6) *Be doctrinally sound.* There should be no doubt regarding the soundness of the teacher doctrinally. He should be in complete agreement with the articles of faith and the **doctrinal** position of the church.

(7) *Be willing to seek lost souls.* Now many Sunday school teachers do not win people to Christ every

week. It may be that a person will be chosen to teach a Sunday school class who has never won a soul. He should, however, voice his desire to be a soul winner and his intentions of becoming one as he is led and trained by the pastor.

(8) *Be converted and be a member of this particular local church.* It might be unnecessary for some leaders to include this in a chapter on requirements for teachers. It might be shocking, however, to some if they knew how many people teach Sunday school in churches and yet do not hold membership in the church where they teach. This is a very unwise practice.

(9) *Attend the Teachers' and Officers' Meetings.* At our church we have a weekly Teachers' and Officers' Meeting. Attendance at this meeting is a requirement for those enlisted to teach. If a person works on Wednesday night, he then is used only as a substitute teacher. Only those who find it possible to attend our Wednesday evening Teachers' and Officers' Meeting are chosen for regular teaching positions.

(10) *Visit the absentees.* It is explained to every prospective teacher that one of his duties is to visit the absentees in his class. The most important absentee to visit is the one who was absent last Sunday for the first time. I have often heard pastors say that the first absence requires a letter or a postcard; the second absence, a telephone call; and the third absence a visit. This certainly is contrary to our philosophy. We feel that a visit for the first absence might prevent the second absence.

(11) *Contact the departmental superintendent on Wednesday night if unable to be in the class on Sunday.* This is a very vital duty and requirement. It is unthinkable that a teacher of the Word of God and a leader of young lives would just casually be absent without notifying anyone at all. It is nearly as unthinkable that a teacher would call late in the week concerning an absence the following

Sunday.   This is practically an unpardonable sin! It should be clearly understood by the prospective teacher that faithfulness is a requirement; but when an emergency comes up or a necessary trip is to be made, the superintendent should be contacted no later than Wednesday evening.

There are other qualifications that perhaps would vary with each local situation, and there are other qualifications that perhaps we should have mentioned with the appropriate notes above.   The important thing, however, is to *have* qualifications and present them clearly and plainly to the prospective worker.

8. *The conversation should be closed with prayer.* The person doing the enlisting should ask God to give wisdom to the prospective worker and thank Him for the nice visit. Before leaving, the prospective worker should be asked to pray for a few days (not more than a week) about the opportunities presented.   It is usually best not to get an answer immediately, but to give him time to solidify his decision and know the mind of God.

9. *Kindness and gentleness should prevail during the conversation.* Some of the above qualifications, duties, etc., may seem to be a bit hard on paper, but in no case should the pastor, Sunday school superintendent, or person who is doing the enlisting be harsh, unkind, rude, or excessively frank.

Following is a typical conversation between the person doing the enlisting and the person being enlisted:

(By Mrs. T. D. McKinney, Director of Literature, who has had the duty of enlisting new workers in our Sunday school)

Mrs. McKinney: Please come in, Mrs. ————. I appreciate your keeping this appointment with me. Won't you sit down here? I'll sit here.

When I called and asked you for an appointment to meet with me, I told you that it is one of my duties to enlist workers for our Sunday school. You have probably guessed that I would like to talk with you about the possibility of working in our Sunday school. Before we go any further, let me tell you that I have asked Brother Hyles for his approval to talk with you about teaching, and he has given that approval. Before we begin our conversation, let's bow our heads now for a word of prayer.

(There is a short prayer asking for the Lord's guidance in conversation and in decision making.)

Mrs. ————, we very carefully choose those whom we wish to work with us in our Sunday school. This is the Lord's business, and we want the right people to work in it. We do not look for people, necessarily, who have had experience in teaching or who think that they are good teachers. Since the Lord can enable us to do whatever He wants us to do, we do not worry whether prospective teachers have teaching ability or not. We are concerned more about finding people who have a concern for getting the Word of God into the minds and hearts of children and adults.

Now I have said that we are not concerned with previous teaching experience when we ask a person to teach in our Sunday school. We are concerned, however, with other qualifications.

There are certain requirements which must be met by each person before he is a teacher, and there are certain duties that each teacher must fulfill.

Let's discuss these requirements and duties for a few moments. We have mimeographed a list of the requirements so that you can see them while we discuss them. (The following form is then given to the prospective teacher.)

(Illustration on next page)

FIRST BAPTIST CHURCH, HAMMOND
TEACHER REQUIREMENTS

1. FAITHFUL ATTENDANCE TO ALL THE PUBLIC
SERVICES OF THE CHURCH.

2. STRICT ADHERENCE TO THE CHURCH'S POLICY
CONCERNING SEPARATION FROM THE WORLD.
(Drinking, dancing, smoking, etc.)

3. GIVING THE TITHE AS COMMANDED IN THE
SCRIPTURES.

4. LOYALTY TO THE ENTIRE PROGRAM OF THE
FIRST BAPTIST CHURCH.

5. FAITHFUL ATTENDANCE TO SUNDAY SCHOOL.

6. FAITHFUL ATTENDANCE TO THE WEDNESDAY
EVENING TEACHERS' MEETING. The meal
begins at 6:00; meeting begins at 6:30.

7. A REGULAR WEEKLY TIME OF VISITATION IN
BEHALF OF THE SUNDAY SCHOOL CLASS.

First of all, we require of our teachers that they be faithful in their attendance to all the public services of the church. Through listening to the preaching of the Word we are constantly instructed in the Scriptures, not only in knowledge but also in Christian living. We have noticed, Mrs. —————, that you are faithful to attend church services Sunday morning, Sunday night, and Wednesday night.

Secondly, we require that any prospective worker in our Sunday school must now be giving strict adherence to the church's policy concerning separation from the world. Naturally, if we are handling the Word of God and teaching how Jesus would have us live, we must be doing all that we can to be clean vessels and to be living as Jesus would have us live. We do not think that you drink liquor or that you smoke or that you dance or that you play cards or that you go to the movies. If you do any of these things and we are not aware of it, then, I'm sorry, we cannot use you on our Sunday school staff. Can you say that you meet this requirement of separation from the world?

Mrs. —————: Yes, I meet this requirement. I do not smoke or drink or dance or play cards or go to movies.

Mrs. McKinney: Our third requirement is that every teacher in our Sunday school be a tither. Our pastor makes it plain that neither he nor any other person in the church office knows how much a person gives, but we believe that tithing is the Bible way of giving. Do you give a tithe of your income to the Lord?

Mrs. —————: Yes, we tithe.

Mrs. McKinney: We require of our Sunday school teachers that they be loyal to the present program of the First Baptist Church. We do not mean by this that they have to blindly follow every opinion that is stated apart from doctrinal beliefs, but that they would never speak against any phase of its work to any other person. Concerning doctrine, we ask that they agree in every point as they have heard it preached from the Bible.

Our teachers must, of course, believe that the Bible

is the divinely inspired Word of God and that men wrote the Bible as they were led by the Holy Spirit.
Now, Mrs. ————, are you in accord with our soul-winning emphasis, our doctrinal stand, and the program of our church?

Mrs. ————:   We agree wholeheartedly with the preaching and the program here.

Mrs. McKinney: Very good.   Now, it goes without saying that we expect of our Sunday school teachers faithfulness in their attendance to Sunday school.   Unless illness prevents or the vacation period includes a Sunday, we expect our teachers to be in their places every Sunday ready to teach their classes.   If for any reason a teacher has to be absent, the departmental superintendent must know, if at all possible, by the previous Wednesday night so that a general teacher can be prepared to take the class.   As soon as it is apparent that he cannot be present in Sunday school, each teacher must let the superintendent know this.

We have a weekly teachers' meeting.   The meeting is held on Wednesday evenings.   We eat a meal together at 6:00 and begin the meeting at 6:30.   We do not require that our teachers be present for the meal, although it is a good idea to plan to come for convenience sake, but they must be present every Wednesday night just as faithfully as they are present for Sunday school.   At the teachers' meeting, plans for the coming Sunday and other future plans are discussed.

The Sunday school lessons are distributed at the teachers' meeting and then the lesson is discussed by the pastor in the hearing of teachers who are in Junior I and older departments.   Teachers who are in the Primary II and younger departments meet individually and discuss the lesson with their superintendents, because there is a little different approach for them to the same lesson material.   After the discussion of the lesson the group divides into a methods session.   A visual aid method appropriate to each teaching level is presented in these groups.

Can you be present at the teachers' meetings on

Wednesday evening?

Mrs. ————: Yes, I can come. I will also be able to come for the meal. What do you do — furnish dishes potluck style?

Mrs. McKinney: It is a modified potluck style. The meat dish is ordered by someone in the church office and the teachers bring salad and vegetable dishes to accompany the main dish. A fifty-cent charge is placed upon the meat for each person. You will be interested in knowing that the entire family is invited to come and eat with us. When the meeting begins, the children and teen-agers have their choir programs so that they are cared for while the teachers have their meeting.

We have one last requirement for our teachers. Because it is mentioned last, please do not think that it is unimportant. It is very important! We ask that every teacher in the Sunday school set aside some time each week for visitation in the homes of his or her pupils. Visits should be made particularly upon those pupils who were absent the most recent Sunday. Can you arrange your schedule so that you will have regular weekly visitation upon your class?

Mrs. ————: Yes, I can.

Mrs. McKinney: Mrs. ————, we would be most happy to have you join the teaching staff of our church. We have an immediate need for a teacher of a girls' class in the Junior II department of our Sunday school. Mrs. Meredith Plopper is the superintendent of that department. I would like to be able to inform her that I have found the teacher that she needs there. May I enlist you to work there and to teach a class of fifth-grade girls?

Mrs. ————: Yes, I would like to teach there.

Mrs. McKinney: Can you start immediately? Will you be able to attend your first teachers' meeting this coming Wednesday evening?

Mrs. ————: Yes, I can be there, and I will gladly begin immediately.

Mrs. McKinney: All right. I will tell Mrs. Sandi Plopper to inform the pastor that you will be there. If there is an emergency of any kind that prevents your coming to that meeting, will you let me know before Wednesday morning?

Mrs. ————: All right, I will.

Mrs. McKinney: If you have not seen the Junior II department, I would like to show it to you now. Would you like to look into it?

Mrs. ————: I think that I know where the department is located, but I have never been inside it.

Mrs. McKinney: Then, let's go look at it. We go this way.

(Upon parting, the enlistee thanks the new teacher for coming and assures her or him that the superintendent will learn of the new appointment. The superintendent is introduced to the new teacher before the teachers' meeting, and the superintendent acts as guide to the new teacher on Wednesday night.)

8. The Teachers' and Officers' Meeting

Any successful endeavor must have a meeting of the minds on the part of its leadership. Any successful company must have meetings of its workers. Such is the case with the Sunday school. Some churches have a monthly workers' meeting. This is definitely not often enough. We have what we call our weekly Teachers' and Officers' Meeting. Our schedule is as follows:

6:00 to 6:30 Meal
6:30 to 6:50 Promotion and Inspiration
6:50 to 7:10 The Teaching of the Lesson
7:10 to 7:30 Instructions of Teaching the Lesson (Instructions are given to teachers of each departmental level as to how to apply Sunday's lesson to the particular grade level involved.)

There are several things that such a weekly meeting will do for a Sunday school. In the first place, it will form a "team" of the workers with the pastor as its captain. A team spirit will develop. Each meeting will become sort of a pep rally and *esprit de corps* will follow. The meeting also gives a specific time for making definite plans for the next Lord's Day. It gives the teacher the inspiration and information and practical how-to-do-it methods for the teaching of the lesson for the coming Sunday.

The weekly meeting also affords the pastor the opportunity of recognizing those who have done good jobs and inspiring those who have not. Classes and departments that are growing receive deserved recognition. Those that are not doing well receive ideas that will help them do a better job for Christ.

This meeting also offers a time for Christian fellowship. It is a time when the saints are happy and joy prevails.

One of the finest things about such a meeting is that it insures a good attendance at the midweek service. Since our Teachers' and Officers' Meeting is conducted on Wednesday evening from 6:00 to 7:30, we have a nucleus of 275 ready to attend our midweek service.

There are many other splendid reasons for a weekly teachers' meeting, and the churches in America that are doing the best job realize this fact.

1. *The meal - 6:00 to 6:30*

The meal is provided for the workers in order that they may be able to attend such an early meeting. Our people live all over Calumet-Chicagoland area. Many of them work twenty to forty miles from home. It would be impossible for them to go home, prepare dinner, and get ready for a teachers' meeting that starts at 6:00 or even 6:30. Hence, they can come from work. Those who possibly can are asked to bring a dish. This can be a salad or vegetable. This means that all the church has to provide is the meat. As the workers come in they place their covered dishes on the serving table. Hot meat is already there as well as bread and other staples. These are also provided by the church. These things are paid for by an offering taken at the end of the meal. We ask each person to give fifty cents if possible. Some do; some don't. Some can; some can't. No pressure is exerted. No embarrassment is present for those who do not or cannot give.

During this thirty-minute period, the people are happy. There is a sweet spirit of fellowship, and our hearts being blended together in preparation for the meeting to follow.

2. *The promotion - 6:30 to 6:50*

Immediately after the meal the teachers are assembled in the church chapel for a period of inspiration and promotion. Each worker is given a copy of the Sunday school *Echoes*. A sample is seen below.

ECHOES ECHOES ECHOES

FIRST BAPTIST CHURCH   HAMMOND, INDIANA   APRIL 17, 1968

We Win Inning 3!

With an attendance of 3,807 last Sunday, we were able to take the third inning by topping the 3,750 of our opponent. Standings in the contests between departments and classes are listed below:

DEPARTMENTS:
1. Beginner II........156.3
2. Beginner I.........144.0
3. Junior III.........134.6
4. Primary II.........133.3
5. Junior I...........132.0
6. Junior High I......131.3
7. Nursery IV.........128.7
8. Primary I.........128.2
9. Junior High II.....123.0
   High School I......123.0
11. Junior II..........122.3
12. High School II.....97.8

CLASSES:
1. Couples.........170.9
2. Bethany.........148.1
3. Deaf............143.8
4. Pathfinders.....137.7
5. Sunbeams........133.3
6. Friendship......116.0
7. Unmarried.......111.8
8. Fidelis.........108.0
9. Men's Class.....107.4
10. Faithful Wrkrs..105.9
11. New Life........104.1
12. Spanish.........95.6
13. Mission.........85.9
14. Pioneer.........84.5

The winning class and department after nine innings will be taken to a major league baseball game in Chicago with the pastor.

LEADERS FOR CHILDREN'S CHURCH-TIME GROUPS:

Nur. Story Hour.......Mrs. William Willey
Beg. I Story Hour.....Mrs. Oliver Douglas
Beg. II Story Hour......Mrs. Merlyn Faber
Pri. I Church..........Mrs. Earl Reeves
Pri. II Church............Mr. John Thrall
Jr. I Church.............Mrs. Lewis Shoaf
Jr. II Church...........Mrs. Rollen Allen

MEAL HELPERS FOR TONIGHT WERE:

Mrs. Walter Ruskowski - Mrs. Vernon Corie

COMING SUNDAY SCHOOL LESSONS ARE:

April 28.....................The Two Rooms
May 5........................The Vail
May 12.......................The Coverings
May 19.......................The Altar
May 26.......................The Laver
June 2..........The Table of Shewbread
June 9.................The Candlestick

MISSION TRIP, BANQUET SET FOR YOUTH

FOR YOUTH

The youth activity for Friday, April 26, will be a trip to the Pacific Garden Mission in Chicago. Meet at the church by 6:30 p.m. to go by bus. There will be refreshments, recreation, and fellowship at the Mission following the service.

Coming up Friday, May 31:
This year's graduation banquet will be held at the Conrad Hilton Hotel in Chicago. All Juniors, graduating seniors, and their dates are invited to come. Cost will be $4 per person.

STANDINGS IN THE CEDAR LAKE CONTEST:

The top ten as of April 14 are:

1-Meredith-Ciesar   6-Norrell
2-Goren-King   7-Smith
3-McCarroll   8-Moffitt-Streeter
4-Sumner   9-Tunis-Vezey
5-Rodgers-Basham   10-Nischik

We then introduce the new teachers that have been enlisted since the previous meeting. They stand and receive an official welcome from the pastor and an applause from the workers.

Each worker is requested to register attendance on the card shown below.

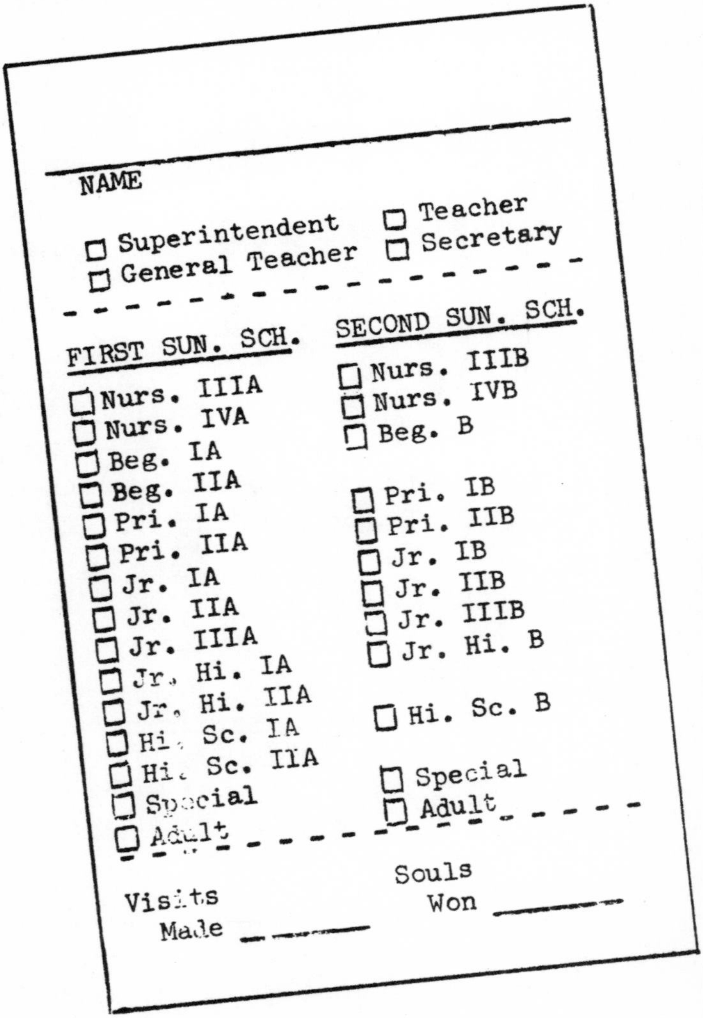

NAME

☐ Superintendent   ☐ Teacher
☐ General Teacher ☐ Secretary

FIRST SUN. SCH.   SECOND SUN. SCH.

☐ Nurs. IIIA   ☐ Nurs. IIIB
☐ Nurs. IVA   ☐ Nurs. IVB
☐ Beg. IA   ☐ Beg. B
☐ Beg. IIA
☐ Pri. IA   ☐ Pri. IB
☐ Pri. IIA   ☐ Pri. IIB
☐ Jr. IA   ☐ Jr. IB
☐ Jr. IIA   ☐ Jr. IIB
☐ Jr. IIIA   ☐ Jr. IIIB
☐ Jr. Hi. IA   ☐ Jr. Hi. B
☐ Jr. Hi. IIA
☐ Hi. Sc. IA   ☐ Hi. Sc. B
☐ Hi. Sc. IIA
☐ Special   ☐ Special
☐ Adult   ☐ Adult

Visits   Souls
Made _____   Won _____

We then discuss the attendance of last Sunday and ideas concerning future plans. Sometimes we inspire. Sometimes we scold. Sometimes we brag. The pastor is in charge of this meeting, and he does his best to instill in the hearts of his workers a desire to do their jobs better. During this period we may exchange ideas. We may ask and answer questions concerning the work. We may set goals or see how close we are coming to reaching our present one.

3. *The Teaching of the Lesson - 6:50 to 7:10*
During this time the pastor teaches the Sunday school lesson. A rather lengthy outline is given to each teacher. See an example below.

Sunday School Lesson
April 24, 1966
Acts Chapter 16

by Jack Hyles, Pastor
First Baptist Church
Hammond, Indiana

THE CONVERSION OF THE PHILIPPIAN JAILER

Aim: to teach my pupils the story of the conversion of the Philippian jailer and the conversion of the first convert in Europe, Lydia.
Point of Contact: A significant passage would have to be verse 9 when the man in Macedonia prayed, "Come over unto Macedonia, and help us." Paul was at Troas and would have gone elsewhere, but the Holy Spirit forbade him to do so. Then came this vision of the man at Macedonia saying, "Come over unto Macedonia, and help us." Since this was a vision, and visions and dreams are so closely associated, ask the pupils something about dreams. Ask them if they ever thought that God spoke to them in a dream. Ask them if they can remember any funny dream they had. Have them very briefly give a detail or two about it. Do not go into length here. Simply have them make a statement like this: "I dreamed one night that I was a horse pulling a milk truck." Then they might think of all the dreams in the Bible and who dreamed them. This, I think, would be a good point of contact.

Introduction: This chapter deals with the spreading of the Gospel into Europe. It is certainly vitally connected with each of us, for the Gospel first went to Europe, and from Europe it came to America. Hence, we owe a great deal to the events of this chapter. Now let us notice the story.

I. THE STARTING OF THE EUROPEAN WORK
    (The first convert was Lydia. Read verses 12-15. Let us notice some significant facts about this story.)
    1. Philippi was a wicked, idolatrous city under the Roman Empire's rule.
    2. Read verse 13. Notice the words, "where prayer was wont to be made." This could be better translated, "the place of prayer." The "place of prayer" is a Jewish phrase. It was used for special prayer places that were located throughout cities where no synagogues were built. If a city had no synagogue, they would build some kind of a wall, usually circular, with no roof, simply under open sky, and almost invariably near or beside a river. This is what is meant in Psalm 137: "By the rivers of Babylon there we sat down, yea we wept." These places were located strategically and were places where the Jews would meet for prayer.
    3. Notice the small beginning of this work. The fact that there was no synagogue leads us to believe that the work was very, very small. In any city where there were ten Hebrews of eminence, there they built a synagogue. You will notice here that only women were present. Simply a little group of women, recognizing their need of God, were gathered in the place of prayer in Philippi. Someone has said, "Great oaks from little acorns grow." God can do a lot with a little. Think of the Gospel as it spread throughout all of Europe. Think of Martin Luther in Germany, John Calvin in Geneva, John Knox and his great revivals in Scotland. Think of Wesley, Whitfield, and the other

great works done in Europe. All of it came from this small beginning. Never minimize little things. It was a little maid who pointed Naaman toward Elisha for the healing of his leprosy. It was a little lad who gave his loaves and fishes for the feeding of the five thousand. It was a little rod that smote the Red Sea and caused the Jews to walk over on dry ground. It was a little stone that felled Goliath; it was a little lad that hurled the stone. It was a little slingshot that the lad used. It was a little Gideon that slew the Midianites. It was a little Andrew who won Peter to Christ. Here we find a little band of women laying the foundation for the great work that has been done in Europe through the Holy Spirit.

4. Verse 14: Here we have the first convert in Europe. Her name was Lydia. She was from Thyatira which, interestingly enough, was one of the cities that Paul had to bypass in obeying the call from the man in Macedonia who cried, "Come over unto Macedonia and help us." Though it seemed like Paul was bypassing Thyatira, one of their citizens was waiting for him at Philippi. Several things about Lydia:

1 - She no doubt started the church in Thyatira.
2 - She was a business woman. Perhaps this is why the Lord led her to be the first convert. She had contacts and met many people every week. She could be a ready witness for Christ.
3 - She was interested in religious matters. Some think she was a Jew and hence came to the place of prayer. Others think that she was a Gentile converted to Judaism, and hence came to the place of prayer. I lean toward the latter. The fact that she left her Gentile idolatry and came to Judaism would lead us to believe that she was seeking the truth. One step that she was making forward was in accepting monotheism, which is a belief in one God. This is so necessary for a person to believe before he is even ready for the true Gospel.
4 - She was a constant source of joy to the Apostle Paul. In Philippians 1:3-5 we read, "I thank my God upon all my remembrance of you, always in every prayer of mine for you (on behalf of you) making request with joy, for your fellowship in (furtherance of) the Gospel from this day unto now." What was this "first day?" This was the day when Lydia was saved. Paul always remembered that experience with joy and delight.

5. Verse 13 teaches us that the women were present. Something we ought not to pass by is the fact that Paul was willing to come and preach to these women. Paul had been a Pharisee and for many years of his early life had repeated every day such words as these: "Oh God, I thank thee that I am neither Gentile nor slave nor woman." He also wrote later, "In Christ there is no Jew nor Gentile, bond nor free, male nor female." What a change we see in Paul's life.

6. We ought to note also the importance of there being a place where God's people gather, whether it is an enclosure near a river or a church on a street corner, God has always had a place for His people to gather for fellowship and praise. This has not necessarily been a gathering for worship, as worship can be done alone, but rather a gathering for fellowship, praise, encouragement, and strength. This teaches us to believe that God would have us get together; hence, we have our churches.

II. SATAN'S ATTEMPT TO FORM AN ALLIANCE (Verses 16-18)
When God begins to work, the Devil wants to use God's power and the success of God's servants, especially if one of God's servants has become famous or well-known or if one of the works has become prosperous. Satan seeks an alliance. This is the case here. A fortune teller, or a false religionist, sought to get the two religions to go together -- Paul's teaching of Jesus Christ and the false religion embraced by this lady. Let us beware of entanglements with those who do not believe the true Gospel. We are not surprised that this temptation came immediately.

III. PERSECUTION
This progression inevitably is followed: First the power of God, then Satan's efforts for alliance, then persecution when God's people refuse to align themselves. This is found in verses 19-24. Paul and Silas were placed in prison. They were in the inner prison, which was dark and deadly and dismal. Their feet were fast into stocks so that there would be no physical comfort in the dark hours. They had been publicly whipped, beaten, bruised, and lacerated. Notice a fact that we have tried to bring out again and again and again. Satan does not persecute us because we pray or because we worship. He persecutes us because we win souls and have spiritual victories.

IV. THE TESTIMONY (Verse 25)
This is one of the great verses in all the Bible. Let us notice a few things
about this verse:
1. Notice the word "praying." The word "praying" actually should be translated
"hymning," which means they were singing the Psalms or some other songs of the
early church. They were rejoicing, testifying, praising God, and singing
psalms.
2. Notice the words please in verse 25: "And the prisoners heard them." The
word "heard" here is much stronger than we find it translated in this verse.
The word "heard" means "listened intently." It is the strongest kind of listening. It implies putting your ear up to the keyhole, bending your ear eaves-
dropping, etc. No doubt these prisoners could not believe what they heard.
It was the talk of the prison. They listened carefully to hear what was
happening. What a testimony. May God help us to have such a testimony.

V. THE DELIVERANCE (Verses 25-28)
God has a way, doesn't He? Right will come out right in the end. However, if it
did not come out right in the end, it is still supposed to be done. Right is
right even though it turns out wrong. But bless God, in the end, it will not
turn out wrong. It may seem wrong for a while, discouragements may come for a
while. Paul and Silas could have said, "Look what standing for the truth got us
into. Look at our condition." They didn't. They had faith that God would deliver
them. God will deliver those who do right.

VI. THE SOULS
After we have refused the alliances, accepted the persecution, given the testimony,
and enjoyed the deliverance, the inevitable thing is souls. Let us notice several
things about the conversion of the Philippian jailer:
1. His question: Verse 30: The word "Sirs" here is a bad translation. It is
the same word that is used in verse 31 when Paul says, "Believe on the Lord
Jesus Christ." The word "Lord" and the word "Sirs" in verse 30 are the same
word. What the jailer was saying was, "Lords, what must I do to be saved?"
He was casting his worship in their direction, believing them to have some
supernatural power, no doubt.
    I think, however, in this place he was not asking for salvation of his
soul. Perhaps he was asking for deliverance.
2. Their answer: What a tremendous time to witness. Paul told him how to be
saved. Here is the one place in the Bible where the question of how to be
saved is answered. Paul is saying here, "Don't call me Lord since Jesus is
the Lord. What salvation you need is not salvation of the body from this
earthquake. You need salvation for your soul." Then he said, "Believe on
the Lord Jesus Christ and thou shalt be saved and thy house."
3. Notice the change in the Philippian jailer.
    1 - He washed their stripes. What a change. His attitude toward the preachers
    was changed. This is the same fellow who last night had plunged them into
    the inner prison, cared not at all for their bleeding wounds, and went off
    to sleep. What a change.
    2 - He took them to his own house. Actually, this is a little stronger. It
    means he took them to his own house and set a table before them. Get the
    picture: He washed the bleeding wounds that he had helped inflict and now
    he feeds the same men that he had tried to starve. Here we see the great
    power of the Gospel, the transforming power of Jesus Christ.
    3 - Verse 33: Notice he is baptized immediately. This same thing is told
    about Lydia back in verse 15. Here in this one chapter we have two definite
    examples of converts being baptized immediately. These had been rugged
    people, too, before. They were the kind that we would want to wait and
    check on. Not so in the Bible. It should not be so now. Stress the
    importance of baptism to your class. If there are those who have been
    saved but not baptized, emphasize their need to follow Christ in believer's
    baptism.
    4 - His entire family was saved. (Verse 33) This had been promised, of
    course, in verse 31.
    5 - He rejoiced in his salvation. (Verse 34)

QUESTIONS:

1. Who was the first convert in Europe?
2. Where was she from?
3. Was there a synagogue in Philippi?
4. What were the group of women gathered by the river doing when Paul came to them?
5. Of what religion was Lydia?
6. In Paul's vision, a man was calling him from what country? What was he saying?
7. What did Paul think of the status of women before he was converted? What did he think of the status of women after he was converted?
8. What did Satan try to do after Lydia was converted?
9. With whom was Paul put in prison?
10. What did they do in prison?
11. Were the other prisoners interested in their testimony?
12. What did the Philippian jailer ask Paul and Silas?
13. Give three things the Philippian jailer did after his conversion to show a great change had been made in his heart.

MEMORY VERSE: Acts 16:31 - ". . .Believe on the Lord Jesus Christ, and thou shalt be saved, and thy house."

Sometimes the pastor will take a few primary children, form a class in front of the teachers, and demonstrate how to teach a primary group. He may do the same thing for juniors or other age groups. The pastor also goes through the outline with the teachers and tells them what he would like for them to stress the next Sunday. It may be that a certain part of the lesson is more appropriate for high schoolers and another part should be stressed to the adults. It may be that a portion of the lesson is not applicable to children. He will make some suggestions as to what to teach each age and how to do it. This teaching is done by the pastor to those who teach juniors, junior highers, high schoolers, and adults. Other trained people do the same for the teachers of primaries, beginners, and nursery children.

4. *The Application of the Lesson - 7:10 to 7:30*

During this time the teachers go to their own departmental level where an expert will teach the teachers of juniors how to apply to their students what the pastor has just taught them. This same plan applies to all age groups. Here visual aids are suggested, applications are given, psychological helps in reaching each particular age level are presented, and in general, the facts which were taught in the previous twenty minutes are made interesting to each particular age level.

5. *Three Outlines are presented each week.*

As seen previously we present an outline to those who teach juniors and up. Still another outline is presented to those who teach primaries. See below:

Elementary Sunday School Lesson
   Exodus 27:1-8; 38:1-7, 29-31.
May 19, 1968

By Erma McKinney
First Baptist Church
Hammond, Indiana

THE TABERNACLE--THE ALTAR

Objects to have:

Square hollow box covered to look like brass.
A mat woven of paper.
"Horns" for gluing onto the corners of the altar.
Glue.
The picture of the lamb.

Introduction to the story:

I'm going to give you a riddle; see if you can guess it. In the Bible we read about a very expensive building. Many things in and about this building were covered with gold. The ceiling was most unusual--it was of cloth. This building was a place for God to meet man. This building could be taken apart and moved. Some parts could be rolled up just like a tent. All parts of it, including its furniture, could be carried from one place to another. What was this building called? Yes, the tabernacle.

Sit real still with good listening ears, wearing tight thinking caps, to hear the Bible story about the tabernacle today.

Telling to story:

Somebody is coming inside the gate that is in the front of the fence. Oh, be careful! Don't get too close to this first thing that is inside the gate. There is fire burning there. This is the altar. Fire burned on the altar in Moses' day. Before fire burned on the altar, God told Moses how to build the altar.

We need somebody to work in a lumber yard today. Remember the Sunday that we pretended to go out and chop down some trees for the walls of the tabernacle? Well, we need some more wood today. We need to get some boards from our supply of wood. Who will quietly raise his hand to volunteer to help me choose some lumber for the building of the altar? (Choose one or more children.)

All right, we need enough boards to make an altar this big. (Indicate 7 and 1/2 feet by 7 and 1/2 feet.) Do you have the boards? Thank you very much. Your work is done now: you may sit down.

Now we need some carpenters who will put together the boards to make a hollow altar like this, but as big as I showed you. (Have a square hollow box. Choose some children to be the carpenters.) Carpenters, let's pound the boards together. Someone lay some boards down to pound them together. Now we'll have to pound some boards together to make the other side, and the other, and the other. There, that's the framework of the altar finished. Thank you. You may sit down, carpenters.

Next, I'm going to put on a brass cover all the way around the outside of the altar. I am also going to put a brass cover all the way around the inside of the altar. There will be no wood showing when I get finished covering the wood altar with brass. This will be called the brazen altar--it will be covered completely and air-tight with brass. It's very important to do a good job.

Inside the altar we'll fit a big brass plate called a grate. (Put your woven "mat" inside your box altar.) The sacrifice was laid on this grate.

On the corners of the altar were things sticking out that were called horns. (While the children watch, glue some projections that are shaped like cows' horns on the four corners of the altar.) These horns were very important. The animal that was being sacrificed on the altar was tied to these horns.

Along with the altar were some tools. There were shovels and pans and other things-- they were all made of brass, too.

Here's our brazen altar. What is it called? This is why there had to be a brazen altar: God said, "I want people to talk to Me. But, people have sinned--they have done wrong. I am holy," said God. "I cannot have sin come into My presence. I must make a way for people to come and talk to Me."

This is the way that God said that people should come to Him: They should kill some- thing so that blood can come out. If there is some blood shed, then people can come to God. But, not just any blood is the way to God. God said, "An animal has to be killed. Killing an animal will be the way that people can come and talk to Me until Jesus comes to earth. After Jesus comes and dies on the cross and rises again, people can talk to Me by trusting Jesus as their Saviour."

(Pick up your picture of a lamb.) "But," God said, "not just any animal will do. You have to kill a lamb, and you have to kill the lamb at the brazen altar of the tabernacle. Just one lamb won't be enough. You have to kill two lambs every day--one lamb in the morning and one lamb in the evening."

Let's pretend that there was a boy named Dan who lived in one of the tents in the Israelite camp. One day Dan's daddy said, "Dan, we have to go to the tabernacle to give a sacrifice for our sins." Dan was pretty excited about this. It was so interest- ing to go stand in the courtyard of the tabernacle near the altar. From this place he could watch everything that was going on. He could even see inside the tabernacle. He knew that he must not go inside; only the priests were permitted to go inside the tabernacle.

"All right, Dad. When can we go?" "As soon as we catch the animal that we must take for our sacrifice." "I'll help you catch him," said Dan. "Which animal are we going to take?"

Dan's daddy became very serious. "Dan, you know that the sacrifice must be perfect. The animal must be young; he must be healthy and strong. It must be under one year old. And it must be a lamb. Which animal do you think that we will be taking?"

Dan looked very soberly at his daddy. He almost did not want to answer his daddy's question--he knew that there was only one animal that would be the right one for the sacrifice. Dan had a pet lamb that he called, "Snowball." Dan's lamb was not yet a year old. Dan's lamb was in perfect health; he was strong and had never been sick.

Dan thought, "Oh, no, I can't take Snowball and see him be killed on the big brazen altar in the tabernacle yard. I love my little pet lamb. He is so cute and so perfect. But, then, if we don't take my pet lamb, what animal will we take? We have to give a sacrifice for our sins." Even though it hurt Dan a great deal down deep inside him, he said, "All right, Dad. I'll go get Snowball and we'll take him to the tabernacle."

God the Father felt bad like Dan when Jesus had to die on the cross. But, Jesus had to die if people were going to be saved from their sins. Now all that we have to do is to pray, really meaning it: "Lord Jesus, I know that You died for my sins. I want You to be my Saviour." We become saved when we tell Jesus this. Let's pray and thank Jesus that He was God's perfect Lamb dying for our sins.

OUR BIBLE VERSE: John 1:29--"The next day John seeth Jesus coming unto him, and saith, Behold the Lamb of God, which taketh away the sin of the world."

Yet another outline is given to teachers of beginners and nursery-age children. See below:

Nursery Sunday School Lesson
    Exodus 27:1-8; 38:1-7, 29-31.
May 19, 1968

By Erma McKinney
First Baptist Church
Hammond, Indiana

THE TABERNACLE--THE ALTAR

Objects to have:

Square hollow box covered to look like brass.
A mat woven of paper.
"Horns" for gluing onto the corners of the altar.
Glue.
The picture of the lamb.

Introduction to the story:

Here in Sunday School we have been talking about a tent church building. What was that tent church building called? It was called a tabernacle. Say that word with me: "tabernacle." There was a fence around the tabernacle just like a fence that might be around your yard.

There's a great big something just inside the fence around the tabernacle. That great big something is called the "brazen altar."

Telling the story:

(Hold the square box.) The brazen altar looked like this. It was covered with brass and was shiny. Inside was a grate. (Put the mat inside the hollow box.) On the corners of the brazen altar were things called, "horns." (While the children watch, glue the horns on the corners of the altar.) God told Moses to build the altar like this. He told Moses to put these brass-covered horns on the corners of the altar.

Do you know what the people did with the altar? The priests would take a little baby lamb. They would kill the baby lamb. The baby lamb would bleed. They would catch the blood of the little lamb in a pan. When the baby lamb was put on the altar, he was tied with a rope that was around these horns so that he could not jump off the altar. Then he was burned up with fire.

Somebody might feel bad to have his baby lamb burned up and killed on the brazen altar. That's how God felt when Jesus had to die on the cross. God felt so bad when Jesus had to die on the cross. But Jesus had to die. Jesus had to take the punishment for our sins. He had to do this by dying on the cross. Before Jesus came to earth, little lambs had to die every day so that people's sins could be taken away from them.

I'm glad that Jesus loved us enough to die for us, aren't you? Jesus was God's perfect Lamb. Jesus is alive and in Heaven now, isn't He? If we love Jesus, He is also in our hearts.

OUR BIBLE VERSE: John 1:29--"Jesus...the Lamb of God..."

6. *The Teachers' Meeting should be conducted with promptness, dignity, and planning.*

It should be a very impressive meeting. It should be comparable to a meeting of the President's Cabinet, the Board of Eastern Airlines, a City Council meeting, or a sales meeting for a big firm. It should be planned well, started on time, and should definitely appear to be the big-league meeting that it really is.

7. *The Teachers' Meeting should not overlap with the midweek service.*

In fact, nothing should overlap with any of the public services of the church. The Teachers' Meeting should end on time, and the workers should come straight to the auditorium for the midweek hour. Loitering should be discouraged. The midweek service should be started on time with all of the teachers and officers in their places.

9. Proper Preparation

There are at least three types of preparation that must be made before a lesson can be successful: (1) the preparation of the teacher, (2) the preparation of the lesson, (3) the preparation of the pupil.

Preparation of the Teacher

It is certainly important that the teacher prepare his lesson. It is equally important that the teacher prepare himself. Much of this preparation is covered in the chapter on "Weekday Duties of the Teacher." Such preparations include living a separated life, having daily devotions, having a family altar, having a pure mind, having the right motives, visiting in the home of each pupil, visiting the absentees, etc. All of these things should help prepare the teacher for the coming Sunday. There are, however, other things:

1. *The teacher should prepare himself physically to teach.* Of course, every Christian should bear in mind that his body is the temple of the Holy Spirit. Consequently, he should keep his body clean, pure, and fit for the Master's use. Several things should be remembered about the care for the body.

  (1) *Proper diet.* The body is only as strong as its fuel. Most people care more about the health of their dogs and livestock than they do their children and themselves. The Christian should realize that the only thing he has in which to serve God is his

body. Because of this he should put only the best fuel in his body. Each Christian should know his own physical makeup as much as possible and should exercise care in his diet. I discovered a long time ago that I could run better without coffee than with coffee and without carbonated drinks than with carbonated drinks. I discovered that there was more energy in a glass of orange juice than in a cola and more stimulant in a spoonful of honey than in a cup of coffee. A person can do more for God on a high protein, low-fat diet, fresh vegetables, and fruit. Fruit and juices should be included in one's diet if he is to be at his best physically for his Lord. I personally am not much of a pork eater.

I also try not to overeat. *"For the drunkard and the glutton shall come to poverty: and drowsiness shall clothe a man with rags"* (Proverbs 23:21). We are reminded to eat everything we eat for the glory of God: *"Whether therefore ye eat, or drink, or whatsoever ye do, do all to the glory of God"* (I Corinthians 10:31). We are to eat with thanksgiving: *". . .and commanding to abstain from meats, which God hath created to be received with thanksgiving of them which believe and know the truth"* (I Timothy 4:3).

Then, too, there should be times when a Christian eats nothing. Fasting is certainly a Bible doctrine. A spiritual fasting enhances not only one's health but also his spiritual power.

"And it came to pass, when I heard these words, that I sat down and wept, and mourned certain days, and fasted, and prayed before the God of heaven." — Nehemiah 1:4.

"Then I proclaimed a fast there, at the river of Ahava, that we might afflict ourselves before our God, to seek of him a right way for us, and for our little ones, and for all our substance." — Ezra 8:21.

"So the people of Nineveh believed God, and proclaimed a fast, and put on sackcloth, from the greatest of them even to the least of them." — Jonah 3:5.

"And when he had fasted forty days and forty nights, he was afterward an hungred." — Matthew 4:2.

"As they ministered to the Lord, and fasted, the Holy Ghost said, Separate me Barnabas and Saul for the work whereunto I have called them. And when they had fasted and prayed, and laid their hands on them, they sent them away." — Acts 13:2,3.

Some good Bible foods are nuts, pulse (vegetables), fish, real bread, quail, goat's milk, meat, figs, corn, honey, and fruit, such as apples, grapes, etc. Now I am not as much interested in telling the reader what to eat as I am in the reader disciplining himself to eat what he eats on purpose. When I am preaching three to six times a day, I find myself using much honey, drinking a lot of orange juice, eating fresh salads, much fruit, and lean beef.

(2) *Proper exercise.* Doctors tell us that it is very important that we exercise our bodies as we grow older. This, of course, can be done through sports such as golf, bowling, or even more active competitive sports. Many of us do not have time, however, or at least do not take time for such activities. I have found it helpful to do ten or fifteen minutes of calisthenics some time in the morning. My schedule is as follows: approximately 500 steps running in place, ten deep-knee bends, ten touching of the toes, ten sit-ups, ten rocker exercises, ten pushups, and a few miscellaneous exercises chosen as needed. Perhaps the most important of these is the running. People who actively participate in some sport may find this unnecessary, but it is necessary to have some

form of exercise in order to be in proper health.

(3) *Proper rest.* Some people require more sleep than others. Some people can operate very effectively on five hours' sleep a night while others require ten. Each Christian should find his own needs. I find that if I can average seven hours' sleep a night, I can operate at peak efficiency. There are times when I do not come close to this. Hence, the seven hours are not needed for me, but to be at my best, seven hours is necessary. The Christian should learn also to relax wherever he is. My wife laughs often about the fact that I can go to sleep anywhere. I sleep while traveling on airplanes, lying on the sofa, listening to the news, sitting up in a chair, etc. Some people find it wise to take a nap each afternoon. If this is done, it should be complete relaxation. The shoes should be taken off, tight clothing should be removed, and complete relaxation should be enjoyed.

There are many other things that a Christian should do in order to keep his body healthy to the glory of God. Discipline is very important in the life of a Christian, and it should be exercised rigidly.

2. *Prepare mentally to teach.* By this we mean the proper preparation of one's mind. To do this one must discipline himself physically. The mind and the body work so closely together that it is almost necessary for one to have a strong body if he is to have a strong mind. We all know exceptions to this rule, but they are exceptions rather than the rule. A successful preacher or teacher should have mental alertness, accumulation, and knowledge. This, of course, requires as much formal education as is wise, proper, and possible. It should also include a general knowledge of facts, especially current events. I read such magazines as *Reader's Digest, National Geographic, Nation's Business,* and even *Better Homes and Gardens* in order to acquaint myself with facts concerning the work and interests of my members. It is always wise for a Christian to have knowledge on various subjects. The reading of a newspaper is also helpful here. Then, too, proper preparation of the

lesson material is highly important.

3. *Prepare spiritually to teach.* Once again, some of this is covered in the chapter on "Weekday Duties of the Teacher." Daily Bible readings, daily prayer, separated lives, etc., are vital for spiritual preparation. However, one should certainly walk in the Spirit more and more as he approaches Sunday. It has long been my policy to take care of personal and church business the first part of the week, gradually steering away from such matters and toward spiritual matters such as soul winning, Bible study, and prayer as I approach the Lord's Day.

Proper preparation would certainly include such things as getting to bed early enough on Saturday evening, getting up early enough on Sunday morning, brushing over the lesson before going to the class, avoiding being rushed on Sunday morning, etc.

Preparation of the Pupil

Not only is the teacher to prepare himself, but he is to prepare the pupil for the lesson. This also overlaps with the chapter, "Weekday Duties of the Teacher," but there certainly are other things the teacher may do to prepare his pupils.

1. *Greet all class members as they come into the departmental assembly and as they come into the class.* A warm handshake, a friendly smile, a little chatting about what the pupil has done through the week, will always make for a better lesson. Remember that Jesus took people from where they were to where He wanted them. When He talked to the woman at the well, He talked first about water and then about the story of salvation. For a teacher to pal with the pupil before the lesson is very wise and certainly prepares the pupil for the lesson.

2. *Meet all visitors before class.* Since the teacher is there early, he should give a warm, friendly, and effervescent welcome to each visitor. He should write down the name of the visitor as well as interesting facts about the visitor that he might present to the class. Such information as where he lives, what church he attends, with whom he came, etc., should be secured by the teacher before the class

or department ever starts. Win the visitor yourself immediately! This is a must!

3. *Properly introduce the visitors in class.* Visitors in a small class should not be required to stand and give their names and addresses. The teacher should have the names already written down along with interesting facts about them. When he informs the class that it is time to recognize the visitors, each name is read as well as the facts about each visitor. The visitor stands and is warmly welcomed by the teacher, president, or some other designated class member.

4. *Try to enlist the visitors as new members.* "Hold what you have and get some more" should be the philosophy of the Sunday school. Somebody has said that the Sunday school should be the easiest thing in the world to join and the hardest thing to get out of. Do not overly coerce the visitors to join, but let them know that you hope that they will and that you would be honored if they do so.

5. *Do not spend over five minutes on announcements and business.* In our pastorates this has been an unpardonable sin. The purpose of the Sunday school is not to plan a social, but to teach the Word of God. Socials should not be planned in class; they should be planned outside of class with only the announcements being made in class. A long, laborious business time will certainly cause the teacher to lose his pupils and cause the pupils to lose their interest.

6. *Take the pupil from where he is.* This is why it is important to chat with the pupils before the class session, visit their homes, etc. This enables us to find out their interests. The lesson should begin with them in mind. Then gradually the teacher moves from their position to his as he teaches the lesson.

Added to these points should be all of those mentioned in the chapter on "Weekday Duties of the Teacher." Don't forget to prepare the pupil!

Prepare the Lesson

1. *Start preparing on Sunday afternoon.* Sunday is the Lord's Day and should be treated as such. After the teacher has finished the lesson this Lord's Day, he should then

look over the lesson for next Sunday during the afternoon. He should continue studying a little bit every day so as to completely lose himself in the lesson.

2. *Read Scripture passages at least ten times.* In order to become well acquainted with the material a teacher should first learn all the facts about the lesson. He should learn the names, the places, the story, etc. This can be done on the first reading. Then he should read the main portion of Scripture ten times, asking God to give him help and teach him the things about the Scripture. When reading the Scripture, write down any thought that comes to mind and take it in faith that God gave it to you. If the average Christian would read the passage of Scripture ten times writing down every thought he gets about the lesson, he would have enough material already prepared to present a good lesson.

These ten readings of the Scripture should be without helps, without a concordance, without a Bible dictionary, and without a commentary.

3. *Read the Scripture looking for Jesus.* Very carefully go through the Scripture looking for pictures of the Lord Jesus Christ. Remember, the Bible is a book about Him! It is a picture of Him. We should always look for Him in the reading of the Word.

4. *Read it looking for proper names, numbers, colors, symbols, types, etc.* It is infinitely more important to teach what the Bible says and what it obviously means than to look too far beneath the surface. However, in the teaching of adults it may be interesting to discuss types, numbers, etc. Especially is it important to look up the meaning of proper names. In the Bible these often have special significance.

5. *Read the lesson with a list of the pupils in hand.* As you read the Scriptures, look at the names of your pupils. See if there is any particular application that should be made to help each of them. This is certainly an important part of preparation. It is easy to build a hospital and forget the patients. It is easy to build a school and forget the pupils. It is easy to teach a lesson and lose sight of the main purpose, which is the applying of the truth to the pupil.

6. *Finally, read the lesson with helps.* Such helps should

include a good concordance (I have used Cruden's through the years), a good Bible dictionary (Davis' and Cruden's are excellent ones), and if possible, a commentary. Notice that we are not finding out what others say about the Bible until we have found out what the Bible says to us.

7. *Read carefully the literature provided by the church.* This, of course, should be a help and not a crutch. In some cases it may be a quarterly. We provide a mimeographed outline for the teachers.

8. *With all of the above accumulation of facts, the teacher then should prepare his own outline.* This probably should be done on Saturday or at least toward the end of the week.

9. *Brush over the lesson again on Sunday morning.* Each teacher should allow himself from five to fifteen minutes each Sunday morning simply to reread his outline and reabsorb the lesson material.

With a prayer on his lips and a prepared body, mind, and spirit, the teacher may then approach his class in order to prepare his pupils for his prepared lesson.

10. The Weekday Duties of the Teacher

Teaching a Sunday school class is more than just a Sunday morning job. It is a seven-day-a-week job. In this chapter we shall discuss at least some of the things that a teacher should do during the weekdays.

1. *Continually study the lesson.* In nearly every Sunday school what the lessons are to be about is known for weeks ahead of time. This allows the teacher to start studying the next lesson immediately after one lesson is presented. So much preparation should be done during the week that the teacher is simply filled with lesson material. He should know much more than he could ever teach in one class session.

2. *Have a daily private devotion.* It is entirely possible for one to be a good preacher and not to be a good Christian. It is also possible for one to be a good teacher and not be a good Christian. In other words, the mechanics of the lesson and the mechanics of teaching could be completely conquered, and yet if the teacher's heart is cold, his teaching will be as sounding brass and tinkling cymbal. Every day at the same time a successful teacher will have a time of private devotion. This should include a systematic reading and study of the Word of God along with a season of prayer.

In addition to this, each teacher should certainly lead his family in establishing family devotions. Some call this a family altar, some call it family worship. Whatever it is called, it should be done. The family should gather around in a family circle, read the Bible, and pray. At our house we sing a song, sometimes memorize a Scripture, sometimes we talk about character building, we all quote together our family motto, and we discuss the Scripture that has been read.

3. *Have a pure thought life.* The Psalmist said, "*Let the words of my mouth, and the meditation of my heart, be acceptable in thy sight, O Lord, my strength, and my redeemer*" (Psalm 19:14). In Proverbs 4:23 the Lord reminds us, "*Keep thy heart with all diligence; for out of it are the issues of life.*" The Lord said of man, "*For as he thinketh in his heart, so is he. . .*" (Proverbs 23:7a). David said, "*Create in me a clean heart. . .*" (Psalm 51:10a). Again the Psalmist said, "*. . .cleanse thou me from secret faults*" (Psalm 19:12b). To be a success in God's work the heart must be right, the mind must be clean, and the heart must be pure.

4. *Have proper motives.* Unselfishness, sincere love for the pupil, and a desire to do all for the glory of God should certainly be the motive of every Sunday school teacher. Of course, he should want to build a big class, but this in itself should not be the main motive. This and other desires should all be subservient to the one desire of serving God and others.

5. *Pray daily for each pupil.* In order to have sufficient love one for another we must pray for each other. Love can never reach its ultimate unless prayer is included. One of the greatest things that one Christian can do for another is to pray for him. Certainly pupils of our Sunday school need to be on the prayer list of their Sunday school teachers. Pray for them and tell them that you do.

6. *Visit in the homes of each pupil each quarter.* There are many things that a teacher ought to know. Uppermost, however, is the knowing of the lesson and the knowing of the pupil. Just to know the lesson material is not enough; the teacher *must* know the pupil. When Ezekiel was called as a captivity prophet and a watchman on the wall, the Lord led him to go where the people were and to sit where they sat for seven days. He could feel what they felt, hunger as they hungered, weep as they wept, and mourn as they mourned. If one is going to be a good leader, he must know the heart of the follower. Because of this, it is imperative that the teacher go into the home of each pupil at

least once each three months. He may find needs that he never dreamed of before.

7. *Visit every absentee.* Remember that the most important absentee is the one that was absent for the first time last Sunday. Remember that absentees are people, and no one ever became a chronic absentee that wasn't absent the first time. They should be gotten back as soon as possible. It should certainly be a part of every teacher's job to visit every absentee every week. If the class is too large for such an endeavor, it should be divided into groups with the responsibility given to group captains.

8. *"Pastor" your pupils.* In these days of population centers and population explosion, churches are becoming larger and larger, making it impossible for the pastor to pastor all of the people. There are simply too many people who need counseling, comforting, winning, helping, and visiting for the pastor to do it all. This makes it vitally important that each teacher pastor his pupils. He should have a personal concern for each pupil and should make this personal concern obvious to them. The pupils should feel that they could bring to him the most intimate problem or burden and that he would wisely advise and hold all in confidence. The teacher should let the pupil know that he is available at his request. Of course, in order to pastor the class properly, it becomes even more necessary that the absentees are visited and that the teacher enter into the home of the pupil regularly. If one teaches junior boys, it would be wise for him to go to the playground occasionally, watch a little-league ball game, find out his boys' interests, play with them, and get to know them. He should get to know their likes and dislikes, their strengths and weaknesses, and their temptations and trials. It seems that in these uncertain days everybody needs help, but there are so few who know how to help. A teacher should be one of these who knows how to help and does so.

9. *Have a monthly class meeting.* The class should play together as well as study together. A little get-together each month is certainly helpful. Maybe the class could take a trip to the zoo, go to the teacher's house for a meal, go down to the corner snack shop for a hamburger, have a picnic, or just have a simple little party. Whatever it is, the

class should provide some recreation for its members.

These are days when the world has everything to offer. Certainly the church should not forget to provide for the needs for the whole life of the individual. What better time could a child have than to get to know his teacher as he plays with him. A monthly get-together is a very vital part of class life. As I look back over my life, I thank God for those Sunday school teachers who prayed with me and played with me.

10. *Make the classroom attractive.* Not all churches have beautiful educational plants; however, the teacher should certainly do the best he can with what he has. In the first place, the class should be as neatly decorated as possible. A nice picture on the wall, a covering for the table, a vase of artificial flowers, and other forms of decoration are certainly in order.

The room should also be kept clean. True, it is the job of the custodian to do this, but the teacher should check before Sunday to see if the room is properly cleaned.

It is also advisable for the teacher to make preparation each week so the classroom will be a little different as if it were prepared especially for that particular Sunday. A simple rearranging of the chairs would be in order or maybe some fresh flowers would help. Maybe it would be nice to have something written on the blackboard. The words, "Welcome, pupils," with the date would let them know the teacher prepared for their coming on that specific Sunday.

One sure way to do the above is to arrive early enough every Sunday morning to check over the room and make certain it is ready for the pupils to enter. It is so important to make the class personal. The personal touch can make the difference between a successful class and an unsuccessful one.

11. *Be a good Christian.* Of course, there are other things that a teacher should do that all good Christians should do. He should tithe, be faithful to all of the services of the church, live a clean life, etc. Teaching is not just a Sunday job. It must consume our lives. It must be of utmost importance to us. The proper kind of Sunday school leadership will instill this in the hearts and minds of the teachers and officers.

11. The Presentation of a Lesson

The teacher has now prepared himself physically, mentally, and spiritually to teach. He has prepared his lesson throughout the entire week. He has arrived early enough to prepare his pupils. We now come to the climax of the week — the teaching of the lesson. This is the purpose of the Sunday school. This is what it is all about. There are several things that he should remember.

1. *Leave all quarterlies and helps at home.* Remember, the Bible is the textbook! The lesson should be taught from the Bible. As boys and girls grow older, they should have memories of a teacher standing with the Word of God before them at Sunday school. How many times have I attended Sunday schools where the Bible was not even present! The teacher just got up and read what some man said about the lesson. The purpose of the Sunday school is to teach what God said, not what man says. Teach from the Bible!

2. *Do not make any pupil read or talk.* Many people quit Sunday schools because they are embarrassed to attend. Some do not read well. Some cannot think on their feet. When asked to read a verse, they decided they would rather not return. When asked to pray, they were completely embarrassed and unable to respond. It is certainly advisable for the teacher to contact a pupil before the class session and privately ask him if he would read a verse, offer a prayer, or make a comment. It should be the law of the Medes and Persians for no pupil to be required to read or talk in the Sunday school class.

3. *Seek limited participation.* Do not ask the pupil to

read a verse and tell what he gets out of it. The teacher is not there to find out what the student gets out of it. The pupils are there to find out what the teacher has gotten out of it through long hours of study during the week. The teacher may review by seeking limited participation. Sentences that the pupils can complete in unison and questions that can be answered in one word without embarrassment are certainly in order. Other than this, however, it is wise to use the lecture method in teaching.

4. *Be the right age for your pupils.* Be sure that you approach them at their right age level. Become an expert on knowing the age of your pupils, their likes, their dislikes, etc. This is very vital in teaching the proper lesson. Many good lessons have been wasted because they were presented in terms which were over the heads of their listeners. This is also true concerning sermons. Jesus always met people on their own level. He spoke of the lost coin, a lost boy, a lost sheep, a farmer, a man going forth to sow, a fellow who got robbed, etc. Simple illustrations that are down to earth and appropriate certainly aid in the teaching of a lesson.

5. *Stay on the subject.* Questions should be answered if they pertain to the lesson, but the lesson should never get away from the teacher. Remember, teacher, you have prepared all week. Be sure you transfer your knowledge to them. It is also wise to remember that teaching is not a display of knowledge, but a transfer of knowledge. Do not get off the subject.

6. *Teach until the final bell rings or until it is time to dismiss.* It is the unforgivable sin in our Sunday school if someone dismisses their class early. We have so little time; let us use it wisely! The public schools have them for five days, seven or eight hours a day. We have them for about an hour on Sunday morning. Let us take advantage of *every* moment and not waste a bit of it.

7. *Make Sunday school seem part of the preaching service.* When I taught a child's Sunday school class, the reason I did not have a closing prayer was that I did not want the pupils to get the idea that there were two services, but rather one. We simply dismissed by saying, "Now we go to the auditorium for the rest of the services."

8. *Use visual aids in the presentation of the lesson.* It is accepted by all experts on teaching that pupils retain more of what they see than what they hear. To be sure, it is important that they hear the Word of God taught. It is also important that their eyes are used in the reception of truth. Of course, in the field of visual aids, we immediately think of the chalkboard. Every class should be provided with a chalkboard, eraser, and an ample supply of chalk.

Many Sunday schools find it very helpful to use flannelgraph in their teaching the Bible. This is especially good for small children, but often it is an expensive item. Because of this it is wise for the teacher to learn to make his own flannelgraph materials. This can be done and is very effective.

The teacher should also be on the lookout for appropriate pictures in magazines, newspapers, etc. It would be wise for a teacher to keep an eye open for pictures which can be used in the teaching of the Word of God. I can still recall one of my Sunday school teachers many years ago taking pictures of liquor ads, tearing them up, putting them on the floor, and stomping on them in an effort to increase our hatred for that which is evil.

There are visual aids, however, which are very seldom recognized as such. The proper use of the hands, the face, and the body certainly add to the teaching of the Word of God. Oftentimes I have regained the attention of an audience by saying nothing, but by simply moving the body. Sometimes even a silent facial expression can be a help. The truth is that silence itself is often a wonderful aid in teaching.

9. *Review and preview.* There is no way to learn without repetition. When a series of lessons are being taught, it is vital that the main points be reviewed each week. At the present time in our Sunday school we are teaching a series of lessons on the Tabernacle. Each week I begin my class by reviewing the main points all the way back to the first lesson.

Then it may help the attendance for the next Sunday if the pupils have a little preview of the next lesson. This often can whet an appetite and be just the thing that tilts the scales toward their coming next week.

12. Promotion

In order to build a great Sunday school much attention should be given to promotion. Occasionally it is helpful to have a special day working for a high attendance. For a number of years now I have led my Sunday school with a ten- to twelve-week spring program and a ten- to twelve-week fall program. Each of these programs is characterized by a number of promotional ideas. While no church or pastor could use all of them, perhaps each church and pastor could use some of them.

1. *Back to School Sunday*

Once each year on one of the last Sundays in September a "Back to School Sunday" is conducted. The following things may be included:

(1) *A gift may be given to each school pupil.* This gift always has some kind of spiritual connotation and is given to each pupil starting to school. One year a ball point pen could be used. A Scripture verse should be printed on the side along with the name and address of the church. There are many kinds of pens. One year we gave away the world's smallest ball point pen. Another year we used one that writes in three different colors—red, black, and blue.

Another gift that young people and children love to receive as a gift is a notebook, or a tablet, or maybe a ruler. Remember, on all of these use the church's name and a Scripture verse. There are many other gift suggestions. One year we gave away five book covers to each pupil with the church's picture and the pastor's picture on the front. Other suggestions can be secured from an advertising specialty company. These are located in most metropolitan areas. If the yellow pages do not reveal such a company, try contacting some corporation that gives Christmas gifts to its customers. These gifts are often secured from such advertising companies.

(2) *Have high school boys perform the duties of the ushers.* In larger churches this may not be advisable due to the complexities of the duties performed.

(3) *Have the special music provided by the school students.* Much care should be taken that the music is proper and well presented. It is usually better to use the older high school students for this.

(4) *Testimonies could be given by school students.*

(5) *A special gift should be given to each school pupil who brings his teacher to the service.* Announcement should be made both in Sunday school and preaching service for several weeks prior to "Back to School Day" informing the pupils of this special gift so they will have ample time to persuade their teachers to attend.

(6) *The schoolteachers of the local church as well as those visiting the services with pupils should be honored publicly.* They should be asked to stand, and each should give his name, the school he represents, and the subject or grade level he teaches.

(7) *An inexpensive corsage could be given to the lady schoolteachers and a boutonniere to the men.* Have the pastor's wife and, if needed, other important ladies pin these corsages and boutonnieres on the teachers. This, of course, would necessitate their coming to the front for special recognition.

(8) *With the teachers at the altar, the pastor should lead in a prayer of dedication for the new school year.* The pastor should ask God's guidance upon them as they help to guide the lives and destinies of our young people.

(9) *The pastor should then ask all school students to
stand, whereupon a special prayer should be of-
‾fered for God's guidance in their lives during the
school year.* In this prayer the pastor should
certainly ask God to give them diligence in their
studies, separation in their Christian walk, and
honesty in their character. A fitting word could
then be spoken by the pastor to the teachers and
pupils, congratulating them upon the beginning
of the new year and assuring them of the church's
cooperation in every right endeavor undertaken.

(10) *The pastor could then bring an appropriate message on a subject such as, " The School and the
Living God."* He could speak of how to enroll
in God's school (salvation), how to be promoted
in God's school (growing in grace), and then
finally the graduation day (when we shall be like
Him).

2. *Teacher Appreciation Day*

This could increase the Sunday school attendance over a
period of many weeks. It has been used very successfully
in spring and fall programs.

(1) *Announce two or three weeks in advance that the
church will have a Teacher Appreciation Sunday.*
This Sunday may be promoted by having each
teacher to have a record attendance and by asking
each Sunday school pupil to help give his teacher
the biggest class ever on Teacher Appreciation
Day.

(2) *When the Sunday comes the teachers should sit in
a reserved section of the auditorium.* The pastor
and other church leaders should speak briefly
concerning the appreciation the church has for the
teachers. Each teacher should stand, give his
name and the department and class which he
teaches.

(3) *A prayer of dedication should be offered thanking
God for the teachers and asking God's blessings
upon them.* This would be a good day to have
near Promotion Day. Perhaps just before Promotion Day would be a suitable time. Through

the months the pupils and the teachers have become close to each other. Now it is time to express appreciation and gratitude. Because of the plans presented in the following points, however, Teacher Appreciation Day should not be scheduled any nearer to Promotion Day than four Sundays.

(4) *A gift should be presented to each teacher.* These should be gift-wrapped and have a card attached. The gifts should be of spiritual benefit to the teacher. A lovely Bible could be one gift. A one-volume commentary of the Bible, a Bible dictionary, a picture with a spiritual theme, or one of any number of items which could have engraved or printed Scripture verses on it would be satisfactory. While the teachers are still standing these gifts should be presented to them.

(5) *The teacher should read the attached card first.* As soon as the gifts are handed out, the pastor or Sunday school superintendent should say, "Now before opening your present, please read the attached card." Words to this effect should be written on the card: "This gift is not to be opened until the class has ——— present in Sunday school." Then it should be explained to the teachers that they will have to put their gifts back on the altar leaving them unopened until they have reached their assigned goals. On the Sunday that each class reaches its goal the teacher then opens the gift. This could be done in the morning service, in the departmental assembly, or at the weekly Teachers' and Officers' Meeting. The message on the card should also inform the teacher that he has only a certain amount of Sundays to reach his goal. These should be no less than four and in larger Sunday schools could extend on to ten or twelve weeks. With every teacher trying to reach his goal every Sunday, and some teachers reaching their goal each Sunday, the plan insures a big attendance for several weeks. Then, of course, when one class has a high day, it helps other classes to have high days. When the adults come

in great numbers, more children come to Sunday
school with them. When the beginners or primaries
do well, they are usually brought by adults, so it
becomes a very effective way to have a big Sunday
school push.

Not only does the aforementioned idea give a big
Sunday on Teacher Appreciation Day, but it guarantees several big Sundays to follow.

3. *Carry the Load Sunday*

The idea behind this is to have a program of several
weeks and asking each department to work hard for just one
week. The idea is to have the nursery break its record one
Sunday, the beginners the next Sunday, the primaries the
next Sunday, the juniors the next Sunday, etc. In larger
churches where there are numerous departments within each
age level, this could become quite a lengthy drive.

(1) *Have a special meeting of all Sunday school workers.* At this meeting explain to them that instead of
asking each worker to work hard for a period of
weeks, this time we are only asking each department to have a "super, colossal day" once during
this big push. (This is exceptionally good for
summer use or winter use during the in-between
times when no special drive is on. It has been
very helpful in preventing summer slumps.) At
this meeting the idea should be presented that on
the particular Sunday that each department carries the load it is to have an unusually high attendance. Not only is it to break its record, but it
is to surpass its record by far. Then the schedule
for the program should be made informing each
worker of the date of his particular big day to
"carry the load."

(2) *A huge sack should be used.* This sack should be
stuffed with paper or some other lightweight substance. It should be ten to twenty-five feet long
with the following words on the side in big print:
"Carry the Load." In the morning service or in
the teachers' meeting the load should be given to
the person who is carrying the load the next Sunday. This superintendent or teacher pretends to

be burdened down with the load as he or she walks
off the platform carrying the sack. The following
Sunday this superintendent should bring the load
back to the platform and give it to the superintendent next in line.   Special recognition should be
given to the superintendent who has carried the
load for the past week and a special challenge presented to the superintendent who shall carry the
load for the next week.

(3)   *Bear in mind that if a department or class doubles
its attendance on a particular Sunday, every department in the Sunday school should be up.* On
the nursery Sunday, the parents would have to be
there.   This is also true on the beginner Sunday.
When the parents have their big day, they will of
necessity have to bring their children.   This is a
way to have a big attendance every Sunday for
several weeks with no one working very hard more
than one Sunday. This would not be as advisable
as some other plans for the spring or fall program,
but it is a splendid way to keep the attendance up
during the summertime or during some other slow
season.

4. *Baseball Game*

This idea has to do with carrying the baseball theme
throughout the entire Sunday school.   This is especially
adaptable to a spring program starting at the beginning of
the baseball season. It can also be used for a drive during
the summer.

A good slogan for such a baseball theme could be, "Winning in every inning." This could be displayed on a huge
sign and placed in the auditorium, departmental assembly
room, or teachers' meeting room.

(1)   *A contest should be conducted with another church.*
Both churches or Sunday schools could choose a
name such as the "Sluggers," the "Tigers," or
some other appropriate name and an attendance
contest should follow for "nine innings." A huge
scoreboard should be placed before the people.
This could be permanent or could be carried in
briefly each Sunday morning. The contest would

last for nine Sundays with each Sunday being an inning, and each person attending Sunday school counting a run. For example, if the Sunday school has 150 in attendance, that would be 150 runs.

(2) *Instead of giving banners or trophies to the outstanding class and department, give baseball bats.* These bats should be big-league quality and should be presented to the department that does the best job of increasing its attendance.

(3) *The departmental percentage of increase should be called the batting average.* An average attendance for a period of weeks should be taken and called the base. Each Sunday the attendance should be compared with the base. The percentage increase is the batting average. The classes and departments having the best increase should be awarded the bats as mentioned above.

(4) *The bats should be presented by a celebrity.* Choose some good-natured person in the church and call him "Slugger" or some other baseball title. Have someone make a uniform for him with the word "Slugger" across the front. In a contest of this sort we used "666" for the number on the back of the uniform. "Slugger" had his hat turned sideways and was a very funny character. He should present the bats to the winning department and class.

(5) *Other prizes could be given to boys and girls doing the best jobs.* These prizes could include baseball gloves, baseball bats, etc. Such items autographed can be secured from big-league baseball teams for a small fee.

(6) *The biggest Sunday of all should be the seventh Sunday.* Each class and department should go all out to have its biggest attendance on this particular Sunday. This could be in a form of a rally day. A Christian baseball player could be invited to give his testimony at such a rally. Naturally, this would be called "The Seventh Inning Stretch."

(7) The winning class and the winning department

could be taken to a baseball game as a prize.
Church buses could be used for this event. It
would be a never-to-be-forgotten experience for the
class and department.

(8) It should be stressed to all classes and departments that they carry out the baseball theme. This
should be done in opening assemblies and in attendance drives in the departments and classes.
This can be a very, very profitable spring or fall
program.

5. *Bible Conference Contest*

We have found this to be one of our most profitable
drives. This has nothing to do with the departments and
classes in the Sunday school, for this is a contest formed on
an individual basis. Two people join to form a team. Each
team resolves to work over a ten-week period to bring visitors to the Sunday school. The winning team receives an
all-expense-paid trip to a Bible conference. It is advisable
to find such a conference that is conducted not too far from
the church, so as not to incur an excessive expense. If the
conference chosen is at some distance, perhaps a church bus
could be used for transportation.

(1) *Several prizes should be given.* If only one prize
is given, the team in the lead could get so far ahead
that the other contestants would lose interest. We
find it advisable to have eight or ten prizes. You
will notice that the prizes graduate downward, but
any prize is worthy of one's work.

(2) *Sometimes perennial absentees could be included
as points in the contest.* For example, someone
who has not been to Sunday school for six months
could be counted. This would not only enable the
Sunday school to reach new people, but reclaim old
ones also.

(3) *The rules for such a contest should be very clearly
explained at the beginning.* A mimeographed sheet
should be passed out to each contestant. The following is a list of rules for such a contest and the
prizes offered.

<u>CEDAR LAKE CONTEST RULES</u>

1. Any person who was not a member of the First Baptist Church of Hammond on March 19, 1967, will count as a visitor. They can be counted as a visitor as often as they come during the contest even though they join our Sunday School or church during the 11-week period. In other words, a person may be brought again and again and count as a visitor each time he comes.

2. Attendance at the Sunday morning or Sunday evening service does not count. A person must be in Sunday School on Sunday morning to count.

3. People cannot be counted who come on their own. By that, I mean a person who just comes to church as a visitor may not be solicited as a member of your group after he arrives at the church building.

4. Any person desiring the use of a bus may secure one by notifying Brother Charles Hand. We will provide a bus for anyone wanting to use one.

5. Deadline for turning in your report each week will be 12:00 noon Wednesday. Reports not turned in by this time may not be counted in the contest. They may not be added to next week's report. You may turn in your report to Mrs. Plopper by meeting her at the Lord's Supper Table after the Sunday evening service or by calling the church office before 12:00 noon Wednesday.

6. Final Sunday in the contest will be May 28, 1967.

7. Contest prizes will be:

<u>GRAND PRIZE:</u>   Tour for two of a mission field--either Jamaica, Alaska, Canada, Bahamas, Mexico, Puerto Rico, or any West Indies Island (or any Bible Conference in the 48 states or Canada).

<u>1st and 2nd:</u>   Cottage, meals and $50.00 in value from the book table or the book store at the Cedar Lake Conference Grounds for the SWORD OF THE LORD Conference week.

<u>3rd and 4th:</u>   Cottage and meals for the SWORD OF THE LORD Conference week at the Cedar Lake Conference Grounds.

<u>5th and 6th:</u>   Large Cottage for the week of the Conference.

<u>7th and 8th:</u>   Small Cottage for the week of the Conference.

(If a prize winner is unable to stay at the Cedar Lake Conference Grounds, he may use the equivalent value of his prize toward any other Bible Conference.)

(4) *Each week's contest standings should be mailed or given to the contestant.* A sample is shown below:

FINAL RESULTS OF THE CEDAR LAKE CONFERENCE CONTEST

1. PHILLIPS. . . . . . 332 ── Room and food for the entire fam-
2. Gehling . . . . . . 330 ──▶ ily for the week at Cedar Lake

3. McKeighan . . . . . 269 ── Cabin and food for the entire fam-
4. Brown-Ahrens. . . . 254 ──▶ ily for the week at Cedar Lake

5. Sharp-Peterson. . . 247 ── Cabin and food for couple for the
6. McCarroll . . . . . 203 ──▶ the entire week at Cedar Lake

7. Hinton-Bair . . . . 174 ── Hotel room for a couple for the
8. Tunis . . . . 164 ──▶ entire week at Cedar Lake.

9. Bailey. . . . . . . 159 ── $25.00 expense money to be used as
10. Grubaugh-Streeter . 148 ──▶ desired at the Cedar Lake Conference

(5) *Once the contest is begun, it should be carried on basically with the contestants.* Little public attention should be given to it. When a prize in a contest is a big one such as this, it is best not to keep it before the people constantly. Weekly or periodical meetings could be held just for the contestants at which time inspiration could be given and a challenge presented. Because this involves a limited number of people, it should not be promoted publicly once it is underway.

6. *Foreign Mission Trip*

For the pastor who knows how to promote and has people who are easily inspired to work hard, this can be an unbelievable drive. It could be included in the Bible conference campaign mentioned above or it could be conducted separately. We have found it beneficial to use the foreign mission trip as a part of the Bible conference contest. It is, of course, the grand prize. To the couple or team of two bringing the most visitors over a period of ten to twelve weeks an all-expense-paid trip is given to some nearby mission field. Churches in the eastern part of the United States could use such places as Jamaica, the Bahamas, Bermuda, etc. Churches in the North could use Canada and Alaska in addition to the ones mentioned before. Churches in the extreme western part of the country could use Alaska, Hawaii, or Mexico. This contest should be heavily promoted and a minimum should be set for the winner. Over a period of ten weeks we have found that the winners usually bring between seven hundred and a thousand visitors. If the contestant does not catch on, it could be a waste of money, so a minimum number should be set in order for a person to qualify to be a winner. If the team which won first place brought only fifty visitors, they would not have earned such a trip.

The trip should include plane fare, hotel, meals, and tips. In smaller churches just the plane fare might be sufficient. With the proper promotion, inspiration, and challenge, this can be a tremendous boost to any Sunday school.

7. *Roundup Day*

Out in the West the roundup is when all the strays are rounded up. After the summer vacation it is a good idea for a church to round up all the "strays" and have a Roundup Day. The following are helpful ideas for such a day:

(1) *Every class and department should be encouraged to have every member present and to bring as many visitors as possible in order to have a record attendance.*

(2) *People may be encouraged to wear western-style clothing.* Those who do should have special recognition in front of the people.

(3) *Cowboy hats could be given to every person attending Sunday school.* Cardboard cowboy hats may be purchased from advertising specialty companies for as little as 10 cents a piece. The name of the church can be printed on the hat along with something like "Roundup Day — 1969." These come in several colors and are coveted possessions by children.

(4) *The entire Sunday school should congregate at the*

front of the church or at some other advantageous place for a giant picture to be made as everyone wears his cowboy hat.

(5) *A pony can be given to the child bringing the most visitors.* In most areas a hundred dollars should purchase a nice pony. Of course, this should be announced for many weeks in advance so as to stir up interest on the part of the children. This pony could be presented in front of the church when the crowd is assembled for the taking of the picture. It is a good idea to have the pony several weeks before Roundup Day. Someone could have him in front of the church each Sunday so the boys and girls could have their appetites whetted as they come to Sunday school.

(6) *As on all special days departmental assemblies and departmental classes should have an emphasis centered around the theme.* Decorations should be used carrying out the western idea of the roundup theme. Opening assemblies, guests, costumes, etc., should do likewise.

8. *Canada Trip*

For a number of years our fall program has been centered around this idea. It is a very simple, yet workable, suggestion. Various contests are conducted and the winners go on an all-expense-paid trip to Canada. Canada is about 250 miles from our city, and such a trip bears with it certain glamour. In other sections of the country, a resort area could be chosen or just a nice trip to any point that would require several hours of driving. Such a drive is conducted in the following manner:

(1) *The teachers and officers of best department or departments over a period of ten to twelve weeks are awarded this all-expense-paid trip to Canada.* In a smaller Sunday school the teachers of the outstanding department could be awarded the trip. In a larger Sunday school more than one department could be included.

(2) *The outstanding adult class or classes could be included on the trip.* In the case of a small Sunday school or small adult classes the entire class might

be awarded the prize. We have found in our Sunday school that the classes are so large that only the teachers of the three outstanding classes win the trip.

(3) *When a church has a bus ministry, the captains of the winning bus or buses could be included.* The most recent such drive that we conducted included the workers of the two outstanding departments, the teachers of the three outstanding classes, and the captains of the ten best buses (we have 60 buses). The trip may be taken on a church bus. Since such a bus will normally care for about forty people, the number of winners should be limited accordingly. It is much more fun to take only one bus and keep the group together.

(4) *Motel or hotel rooms should be reserved in advance.* In some cases two to a room is wise. Sometimes even four to a room will be acceptable. Reservations should be made in a nice motel or hotel.

(5) *The hotel should have a private dining room large enough to accommodate the entire party.* This will enable the group to sing choruses and have testimonies, Bible studies, etc.

(6) *The tour can start at noon Monday and end at noon Wednesday.* This enables the group to arrive at the destination in time to have an evening meal and arrive back home in time to prepare for the Wednesday evening service. The drive should be no longer than 4 or 5 hours and should be well planned.

(7) *Activities should be planned in advance.* We have found it very nice to have stewardesses on the bus. Two young ladies can arrange personally improvised stewardess uniforms (or even make their own) and take along such things as magazines, chewing gum, box lunches, and other surprises that would help in making the trip enjoyable.

Tuesday should be a full day. It could begin with breakfast at the hotel, sightseeing in the morn-

142   THE HYLES SUNDAY SCHOOL MANUAL

ing, lunch in a nice restaurant at noon, and the afternoon given for rest and shopping. Recreation could even be a part of such a trip, and the highlight could be a lovely meal in an exclusive restaurant either Monday or Tuesday evening. This should be a dress-up occasion.

(8) *The pastor should accompany the group.* This gives the pastor and people an excellent opportunity to know each other better. This actually adds a new dimension to the pastor in the eyes of his people. The pastor should enter into the fun and should be a definite part of the group.

(9) *This idea can be used for any type of contest.* One well-known pastor was wise when he gave such a trip to each person who brought a hundred visitors for a period of several weeks. Regardless of the type of contest that a church uses, the idea can be a successful one, and it will grow in its usefulness each year as the people come back and report of the good times they have enjoyed on such trips.

9. *Valentine's Day (Broken Heart Sunday)*

This is just a simple little idea that can be used in any size Sunday school. Cut out a big, red heart for each class. Then cut the heart into pieces sending each member of the class a piece of the heart. The idea is for each member to bring his piece to the class Sunday and put together the big heart. The pieces are placed over a black paper heart. If all are present, they have prevented the class from having a black heart or broken heart. If the members are not all present, then the heart is broken and a portion of the heart is black. Each class may display before the church or the department the condition of its heart after it has been put together. The biggest heart will win a prize.

A letter can be sent to the members with such statements as, "Don't break our heart," "Have a heart," "Be big-hearted," "Put your heart into the Sunday school" and "Bring your heart Sunday so that we will not have a broken heart."

10. *Christmas Cards*

During the summer months an order of Christmas cards

can be made. Twenty or thirty can be in each box and the picture on the card can be a picture of the church or maybe even the church and pastor, or the pastor and family, or some other item of interest. The year that we used this idea, we had a picture taken of the interior of our auditorium. Poinsettias were purchased and the picture was taken in color. The cards were received in time for public display before the fall program began. Any person who brought as many as ten visitors during the ten-week fall program received a box of the Christmas cards. These must be very lovely, and should be ordered in plenty of time to stir the interest and whet the appetites of the people.

11. *Free Books*

As soon as a Christian book is published that would be of interest to all the people or even to a majority of the people, it could be used in the same way as the aforementioned Christmas cards were used. When a person brings a visitor per Sunday over a period of Sundays, he receives the book. The book should be purchased in plenty of time for proper promotion and inspiration.

One year we ordered some little, black Testaments with the outline of our church building engraved in gold on the front. This happened to be our 75th Anniversary. We had the following engraved in gold underneath the church building: First Baptist Church, Hammond, Indiana, 75th Anniversary, 1887-1962. Each person averaging one visitor a week for seven weeks received a Testament. Of course, the offering that the visitors brought more than paid for the expense incurred.

12. *Vacation Bible School Sunday*

This could be conducted the Sunday prior to vacation Bible school or the Sunday immediately following vacation Bible school. This simply extends vacation Bible school by a day and gives the Sunday school the privilege of sharing in the good attendance. This can be in the form of a big rally for all the children of vacation Bible school age. It could also be enrollment day. Interest should be stirred in the hearts of the boys and girls so as to create in them a desire to attend vacation Bible school. If this rally is conducted after the Bible school ends, then it should be announced throughout the entire week or weeks in such a way that will instill in the children a desire to be present. We have found it best to have such a rally on the Sunday preceding vacation Bible school.

We have unusual Bible school characters such as Silly Billy, the ugliest boy in all the world; Phooidini, the Gospel magician; the Old-Timer, who is over a hundred years old and has never missed vacation Bible school; Pee Wee, who is a big fat boy; etc. At the rally these characters are introduced and the children are shown samples of what they may expect at Bible school.

Not only does this increase the vacation Bible school attendance, but it also guarantees a large Sunday school crowd at least one more Sunday out of the year.

13. *Matthew Sunday*

While preparing a message on the conversion of Matthew, I was impressed with the fact that Matthew had a feast in his house and invited the publicans and sinners to attend. This feast took place upon his conversion. It seemed to me that Matthew was wanting to tell the publicans and sinners about Jesus Christ and the salvation he had found through Him. This led me to have a Matthew Sunday. This is the Sunday when all of the people in the church are asked to round up their old crowd and bring them to Sunday school and church. Since Matthew gave a feast for publicans and sinners, we encouraged our people to prepare a big Sunday lunch or picnic to which they could invite the unsaved people with whom they used to run. We gave a free book to every family that prepared such a meal and invited the old crowd to Sunday school, preaching, and lunch.

One by one they came to the First Baptist Church bringing their unsaved friends with them. Over ninety of these were saved as the power of God met with us. Matthew used it with success. The First Baptist Church of Hammond used it with success. May it be a help to many others.

14. *Couples' Rally — Men's Rally — Ladies' Rally*

Approximately once each year I like to talk very frankly to the married people of our church. Sometimes it is in the form of a Couples' Rally, where I speak to them concerning their responsibilities as husbands, wives, mothers, and fathers. At such a rally the pastor may want to give a picture of himself and his wife to every couple who attends.

Eight-by-ten reprints can be ordered in great volumes at about 8 cents to 10 cents apiece. At the rally some couple should sing a duet, and then the pastor should talk very frankly to the husbands and wives.

Some years we have a Ladies' Rally on Mother's Day and a Men's Rally on Father's Day. Special gifts can be given at this rally. On one occasion we ordered ball point pens which had little corsage-like, artificial flowers on top. We placed these in a huge styrofoam board and called it the "World's Largest Corsage." On each pen the following words were printed: "Happy Mother's Day—1966, First Baptist Church, Hammond, Indiana—Jack Hyles, Pastor." At the close of the service each mother came and picked her "flower" from the corsage.

For the Men's Rally Praying Hands "tie tacs" could be used.

15. *Bus Contest*

For a church which has church buses a bus contest will always work if it is properly promoted and planned. A special event is given as a prize to the winning bus or buses. One year we took the winning bus to a little airport nearby, chartered two planes, and gave everybody a free plane ride. All of the time a picnic was going on on the ground for those awaiting their plane ride. A trip to a ball game, an all-day trip to an important place, such as a state capital, or one of any number of similar ideas would be of great appeal to the bus passengers.

There are also ways to have Sunday-by-Sunday contests between the buses. The best bus or buses may be served ice cream on the way home. They may go by the Dairy Queen stands and be served ice cream on the way home. There are many other ways a bus contest may be utilized for the increasing of the Sunday school attendance. During such a big drive appropriate things are given out that have to do with the Sunday school lessons. If the Sunday school lessons are about fishing for men, then goldfish in plastic bags filled with water can be given to the bus children. Bear in mind as we have mentioned before that all prizes should have a spiritual connotation or should be advertisement for the church. All of the prizes that have been mentioned in this chapter have had to do with spiritual enrichment, Christian testimony, or church publicity. We do not use on a churchwide basis prizes that have no connection with the church or spiritual matters.

16. *Christmas Sunday*

This is usually a difficult time for a Sunday school. Because of this we like to have something special each Christmas. The pastor could land in front of the church in a helicopter with Testaments for each child. If possible, each child's name could be imprinted in gold on the cover of his Testament. This would certainly draw a big crowd. Sometimes just the Testaments could be used without the fanfare. Don't give up on holiday Sundays. Fight the Devil in his own back yard. Don't give him the victory in the seasons of the year which should be the best for the Lord's work.

A good thing to use on Christmas Sunday would be a Scripture text calendar with a picture of the church on it. A very attractive calendar could be printed which could be used as a prayer reminder through the year.

17. *Giant Picture Sunday*

Once each year the Sunday school should have a mass picture taken of its entire attendance or enrollment. We have found it helpful to use this picture on our church letterhead, church envelopes, newspaper ads, and in other advertisement. For several weeks in advance we announce that a picture is to be made and that a free picture will be given to each person who attends on that particular day. The names of the people attending should be taken and the picture should be mailed to them later or given to them at Sunday school at a later date. It should be announced again and again that the picture is to be used for many advertising purposes. Promises should be received from the people that they will be present for the occasion.

18. *Helium-Filled Balloons With Gospel Tracts*
This idea can be used with the previous one, or it can be used on its own. Balloons can be purchased with the name of the church printed on them. They can be filled with helium and released at the same time in front of the church. This can be done at the time of the picture and the balloons could be seen in the picture. Attached to the balloons should be a gospel tract with a place for the person to sign who accepts Christ as Saviour. There should also be a card with the following words:

> My name is ——————————. I attend the
> —————————— church in —————————.
> If you will return this card to me at my church
> address, you will receive a gift and so will I. If
> you have never received Christ as your Saviour
> and are willing to do so now, please sign the
> enclosed tract and return it with this card.
> Name: ——————————————————
> Address: ——————————————————

19. *Picture-Taking Sunday*
Once each year the entire Sunday school should have a Picture-Taking Sunday. This could be incorporated with the mass picture mentioned above. A picture of each class should be taken on Picture-Taking Sunday, and the pupils should be given the opportunity of purchasing copies. The best classes or departments could be awarded free copies. People love to have their pictures made. They will come for such a day. Using this idea annually it is entirely possible that a person could grow up having an album which would include a picture of every Sunday school class that he has attended.

When the pictures of the babies are taken, they should be taken in color with a Polaroid camera or some other good camera using color film. Some nice background could be prepared and a doll or teddy bear could be put into the baby's lap and the picture presented as a gift to the parents.

20. *The Awarding of Banners, Etc.*
During any contest it is good to give weekly awards to the outstanding classes and departments. We mentioned

previously the awarding of baseball bats in the baseball drive.   Banners are always advisable.   The "Awful Cup" or "Lousy Cup" is a good one.   To make such a cup you take a tin can or bucket, turn it upside down, put a funnel through the top, and attach bent spoons for handles.   This looks like a trophy.   Beautiful trophies can be presented to the best department and class, and the "Awful Cup" or "Lousy Cup" can be presented to the poorest one.

One year we awarded a character named "Ezirp Yboob" to the poorest department.   ("Ezirp Yboob" is booby prize spelled backwards.)   He was a fellow six feet tall, stuffed with all kinds of junk and dressed up in a suit of clothes. He was a real character and was awarded publicly to the poorest department each Sunday.   People love to be first place and recognized as such.   It is amazing how hard they will work for a little recognition for their class or department.

21. *Shut-in Sunday*

This is especially good for churches with large Sunday schools and membership.   Transportation should be provided for every shut-in who could attend the service.   Ambulances, wheel chairs, hospital beds, etc., can be provided to make it possible for those who normally cannot attend the services to be present on this special day.   The shut-ins should be recognized in the public service. They should receive some kind of gift, such as a nice book, plaque, or some other expression of love and appreciation.   A noon meal could be planned for those who are able to stay.   This gives honor to those who deserve it and brings some sunshine to the people whose days are normally dark.

22. *The Largest Sunday School Idea*

Everybody likes to be a part of something that is the largest or the greatest.   Perhaps your Sunday school could try to be the largest in the state, county, city, or the largest in a section of the city.   Let your people know that you are striving to become that, and then work toward it.   Have some little inexpensive felt pennants made with the picture of your church on it and put on it such words as "The largest Sunday school in Lake County."   Have a ten-week push to become the largest Sunday school in the county.   On the big kick-off Sunday, give out the felt pennants to all who

attend.   Keep the thought before your people constantly
through the program.   Be striving to be the largest.   Most
anyone will rally to this incentive.

23. *Charm Bracelet Idea*

Find a little bracelet with ten religious charms.   On the
first Sunday of the drive give the child the bracelet.   On
the second Sunday, the first charm; the third Sunday, the
second charm; etc.   The idea, of course, is never to miss
a Sunday during the entire push.   Especially is this a good
idea in working with children.

24. *Church License Plates*

In many states only one license plate is sold for the car.
In such cases the front of the car may be used for church
license plates.   These may say simply, "We attend the
First Baptist Church, Hammond, Indiana."   They can be
passed out on a big Sunday.   This not only enables you to
have a big crowd on a given Sunday, but your church is
advertised all over the area.   Each car becomes an advertisement or a signboard for the church.

25. *Pastor Speaks to Departments*

Some pastors find it profitable to make an annual visit
to each department or class.   Especially is this good for
younger children.   To them the pastor is really somebody
and they can get to know him better by having him visit
with them.   For many years I did not teach a Sunday
school class in my pastorates.   During these years I made
an annual trip to each department and class for a little
five-minute, get-acquainted visit.   For the years that I have
been teaching a Sunday school class of my own I simply
stay available to make five- or ten-minute visits in particular departments.   When I do make such a visit, I leave my
class about ten minutes early.

26. *The Giving of a Financial Allotment to Each Department for a Spring or Fall Program*

We ask in our church that each spring and fall program
be promoted on three levels: a churchwide basis, the departmental basis, and class basis.   In order to encourage
the departments to promote on their own, apart from the
churchwide push, we allocate approximately $25.00 to each
department for a twelve-week program.   This money may
be used by the department for their own promotional pur-

poses. Some churches find it wise to put this in the annual budget, giving each department a stipulated amount to spend for the annual promotion of its program.

27. *Pack-the-Pew Day*

This is an old, and yet, effective way to get a crowd. Give each person a pew and have them promise to fill it for the big rally day. Put the name of the person on the end of the pew and make some little reward and give some recognition to those who fill their pews. This is good, not only for a Sunday school push, but for a big night in a revival meeting, or any special occasion.

28. *Old-Fashioned Day*

Once each year our churches through the years have declared their belief in the old-fashioned Gospel by having what we call Old-Fashioned Day. On this day we display a collection of antiques, use a pump organ for the music, pass hats instead of plates, use an old-fashioned mourners' bench covered with quilts, and use coal-oil lamps and lanterns for the light for the evening service. The people wear old-fashioned costumes, etc. (For a more detailed explanation of Old-Fashioned Day see the author's book, *How to Boost Your Church Attendance,* published by Zondervan Publishing House, price $1.95.)

29. *The Birthday Anniversary of the Church*

Many churches find it wise to celebrate their birthday in a big way. A huge birthday cake is purchased. Oftentimes the cake is in the shape of a Bible, a cross, the church building, or some other interesting design. Candles are sent out to the Sunday school pupils. Each one is asked to bring his candle on the birthday for the birthday cake. Birthday party invitations are sent out to the pupils, and sometime during the day the cake is served with coffee or soft drinks. Special guests acquainted with the founding of the church or the early days of the church history can come and tell about the early experiences that the church enjoyed.

30. *Baby Day*

One of the highlights of the year for many churches is the annual Baby Day. There is the Baby Day parade with the parents carrying their babies around the auditorium while the organist plays, "Jesus Loves Me, This I Know." Special letters are sent out to each baby. Pink corsages are presented to all mothers of little girls and blue corsages to all mothers of little boys. Oftentimes pictures are taken of each baby and given as a gift to the parents. The nursery workers are honored. There is a service of dedication for the babies. The pastor simply asks the parents to bring the little ones to the altar, and he has a prayer for God's blessings upon each of them. There can be a reserved section in the auditorium for the parents, and a special sermon could be given by the pastor. (For a more detailed explanation of Baby Day see the author's book, *How to Boost Your Church Attendance,* published by Zondervan Publishing House, price $1.95.)

31. *Homecoming Day*

Homecoming Day is usually conducted in our church on the Thanksgiving weekend. Because of the holiday many people find it convenient to go out of the city. Many of them, however, will stay at home and invite their own friends and relatives to come spend the holiday with them if there is something special at the church. This is a good time for Homecoming Day. Letters advertising the event are sent to all of the people. Former members of the church are contacted with a special invitation. Each family of the church brings a lunch and the noon meal is spread out-of-doors. (In some areas of the country it would be too cold for this during the Thanksgiving season; hence, an earlier date is more acceptable.) Following the morning service there is dinner on the grounds followed by an afternoon service. At this service the old-timers are recognized and other special guests are introduced. A song fest is usually advisable here as well as a message by some well-known speaker. Testimonies as to what the church has meant in the lives of the people are in order at this special afternoon service. If possible, former pastors could be introduced at such a service.

32. *Record Breaking Day*

"Record Breaking Day" can be used to great advantage almost anywhere in the country. Letters are sent out to all of the people advertising it. It should be publicized in the church bulletin and also from the pulpit for several weeks in advance. Display a phonograph record on the platform or some place where it can be noticed. Over the record write the words, "SUNDAY SCHOOL." The previous record attendance should be announced and then a challenge should be made for the people to break this record. On "Record Breaking Day," when the announcement is made that the record attendance has been broken, the record on display is broken over the Sunday school superintendent's head. The pupils will work hard just to see this done.

33. *Good Neighbor Sunday*

An opportunity to gain many good prospects is "Good Neighbor Sunday." Ask each member to bring as his special guest a neighbor, and then have them to stand and introduce their guests in the service. It could be explained that a neighbor might be anyone who lives within a fifteen-mile radius of the church. A gift could be given to anyone who brings his neighbor and a nice gift such as a nice Bible might be awarded to anyone who brings as many as fifteen or twenty neighbors. The pastor might then preach an appropriate sermon such as "Who Is My Neighbor?" — the Good Samaritan story.

34. *Fruitful February*

"Fruitful February" could be one of the most profitable ideas. We have found it to be very successful. First, we cut down three medium-sized trees and placed them in containers of soil and put them in the auditorium. We called one tree an "apple tree," which represented the Sunday school. Another tree was called a "pear tree" and represented the youth group. The other tree was an "orange tree" and was used to represent the Wednesday midweek service. The containers were then covered with red, yellow, and orange crepe paper.

Apples, pears, and oranges were mimeographed on red, yellow, and orange construction paper, and on each was a place for the person to sign his name. They were given to the Sunday school and youth workers to cut out, and it was also their job to get everyone signed up who would promise to be in Sunday school, youth meeting, and the midweek service every Sunday or Wednesday during the month of February. When they promised to come to Sunday school every Sunday in February, their red apples were placed on the apple tree. When they promised to be in the youth meeting every Sunday in February, their yellow pears were placed on the pear tree, etc. Every member of the family would sign up and the apples, pears, and oranges were strung on the "trees" in the auditorium. Of course, as the people signed the fruit, it was interesting to see the "trees" become filled with fruit. Letters should be written to the members stating that if they have not already signed up to be faithful to all of the services of the church, they should sign the enclosed apple and bring it back to Sunday school the next Sunday. The pastor should start several Sundays in advance promoting "Fruitful February" so as to build the attendance for the entire month. After having been faithful to all of the services for four weeks in succession, most of the people would have developed a good habit and then continue to be faithful.

35. *Contest by States*

In some churches, especially in metropolitan areas, people from many different areas attend the services. In such a case, there could be a contest for several weeks between the people born in different states. In such a contest at the First Baptist Church of Hammond, there was a group from Kentucky, a group from Northern Indiana, a group from Southern Indiana, another group from Northern Illinois, another group from Southern Illinois, another from Alabama, another from Tennessee, one from Ohio, one from Michigan and one from the Southwest (Texas, Oklahoma, New Mexico, etc.). One group was composed of those born inside the city limits of Hammond, and one was a Greater-Chicago group. These groups may bring anyone from anywhere to the contest. The workers are simply chosen from the various states.

The flags of the states are brought in as well as a plant of the flower of each state. The song of each state should be mimeographed. For the winning state each Sunday the flag should be raised, the flower displayed, and the state song sung. The captain of the winning group could receive an all-expense-paid trip to some Bible conference in his state. There are many other ramifications of this same idea that can be used in the enlarging of the Sunday school and in the helping of the spring or fall pushes.

Certainly no one person would agree with all of these ideas for special occasions, but we will be grateful to God if a few of them might be helpful to churches across America so that the attendance might be increased, and that more souls might be brought to Jesus Christ. Some will no doubt think that the ideas presented are too sensational. Others will no doubt add more color to them. Take whatever is usable and suitable for you and use it for the glory of God.

Note: There are other ideas for big days and special occasions presented in the author's book, *How to Boost Your Church Attendance,* published by Zondervan Publishing House.

13. The Beginner Department

(Written by Mrs. T. D. McKinney, Superintendent of the Beginner II Department of the First Baptist Church, Hammond, Indiana. Mrs. McKinney is also on the church staff as Director of Literature.)

Years ago I was explaining to a friend in another city that I worked in the Beginner Department of a Sunday school. The reply was: "I suppose working in a department of this age is nothing more than a baby-sitting job."
I replied, "Oh, no. We teach preschool children. Children of this age ought to be taught as much as children in school--and they *can* be taught. As soon as the child reaches his second birthday he is promoted into the Nursery III Department, where he listens to a story and learns songs. He is taught the Word of God in the Sunday school. Since the procedure followed in both the nursery and beginner departments is much the same, everything in this chapter, unless otherwise indicated, can be applied to ages two through five, or from the time the child reaches his second birthday until he enters first grade in elementary school.

Why Teach Preschoolers in the Sunday School?

The operation of these departments is based upon two main principles: letting little children come to Jesus and avoiding in any way offending them so that their faith in Jesus might not be destroyed. Remember the story found in the 10th chapter of Mark. Jesus had been discussing with grownups some very important, weighty doctrinal questions. Suddenly people started bringing their children to Jesus. Perhaps some of these people had been in the crowd when Jesus took a little child and put the child on His knee as an object lesson. Jesus had said, "See this little child? Unless you become like him you shall not enter the Kingdom of God. His faith is not obstructed by any doubt or reservation. He has pure humility. He is not coming to Me on any merit." Jesus loved little children.

As the parents came, each with the determination that Jesus would touch and see his child, the disciples said, "Oh, no, no, don't bring the children to Jesus. Don't bother Him with them. They are unimportant and very insignificant in our society. Can't you see we have been discussing very important things?"

When Jesus saw the disciples trying to hold the children back from coming to Him, He was much displeased. He said to the disciples, "You let the children come to me. Don't you tell them not to come." Jesus reached out to the children, took them into His arms, and blessed them.

As soon as the child has seen Jesus and has learned to love Him, then we ought to be careful in our teachings and in our operations of the Sunday school never to do or say anything to disturb his faith in Jesus. Jesus said in Mark 9:42, "*And whosoever shall offend one of these little ones that believe in me, it is better for him that a millstone were hanged about his neck, and he were cast into the sea.*"

Thus we approach the Nursery and Beginner Departments with a real sense of responsibility and obligation to the Lord to do the very best job that we can do.

What Is Needed Most in Reaching Little Children in the Sunday School?

Prayer is needed most. Every plan, every procedure, and every activity ought to be saturated with prayer. We need love. We need understanding. We need the power of the Holy Spirit in conducting our departments for our little children. "Lord, teach me to love the noisy child as well as the quiet child. Teach me to love the little child that might have dirty hands as well as the little child who is absolutely clean and beautifully dressed. Help me to understand what they are thinking and how they feel and how they are reacting. Help me to remember what it was like to be a child. May each child under my care in the Sunday school someday truly learn to love Jesus and to turn his life over to Him." This is the ultimate accomplishment of our task in teaching little children—that his entire life might be turned over to Jesus.

What Facilities Are Needed?

Let's start with the room. The Sunday school room for preschool children need not be luxurious, in fact the more simple the better. The room must be attractive, clean, and bright. Individual classrooms are not needed for preschool children. The entire Sunday school hour is conducted in one room with all of the children together. The room should be furnished with a piano, chairs and tables of comfortable size for the children, a story rug that can be a remnant of carpeting or an inexpensive quilt spread on the floor, sturdy flannelboard, a chalkboard, bulletin boards, and a small teaching table or stand for use while conducting the department.

In addition to furnishings, there is need for a large double or triple-door closet in each room. In the closet are shelves for holding all supplies. Whenever any teaching aids are not in use they are stored here.

Other necessary supplies are handwork needs: construction paper, brass fasteners, glue, Scotch tape, scissors, etc. Every preschool department should also have a constant supply of paper tissues for wiping noses, and a bag of custodial absorbent material for sprinkling on the floor, table, or chair where a child has had an "accident" or has become ill. The departmental workers should know where a custodian is or where his brooms, etc., are in case they are needed. (It is very rarely that problems like this arise, but when they do, they should be taken care of quickly and in a sanitary manner.)

Some underprivileged children come without stockings, even in the coldest winter. A supply of children's stretch socks has been useful many times. The teacher quietly and nonchalantly puts them on the child's feet in such a way so as not to embarrass the child.

Now decorate the room. Change the decorations at least four times a year, either corresponding with the seasons of the year or corresponding with the particular program which is being conducted, or perhaps a combination of the two. Children love pictures on the bulletin boards — pictures that illustrate what children do and pictures that set a gay, happy mood. There are some paper plates that have funny cartoon animals drawn on them. Hang pretty decorations from the ceiling or from the light fixtures. This makes the room come down to the child's size, and lends more color and attractiveness. Whatever decorations are used, keep them clean, pretty, and uncluttered. Change them often. Seeing the children's reaction as they enter a pretty room and hearing their comments about our pretty room is indication enough that the giving of time, thought, and some money is worth it.

Consider very carefully the arrangement of the room according to the number of children that will be in the room, the number of tables and chairs and the space they will take, and the space allowed for the story rug. The following is a suggested diagram for a room arrangement for the preschool Sunday school department.

(Illustration on next page)

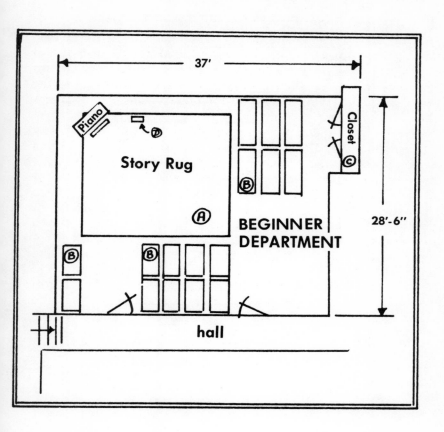

A. Story rug
B. Tables
C. Closet
D. Speaker stand

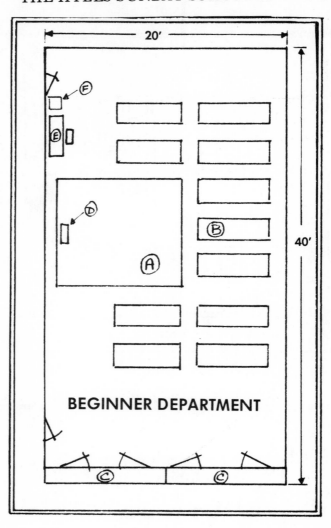

BEGINNER DEPARTMENT

A. Story rug
B. Tables
C. Storage
D. Speaker stand
E. Piano
F. Secretary table

There is no merit whatsoever in setting up what some people call a worship center or interest center. Just by setting the Bible before the children, we will not create in them any kind of desirable attitudes, behavior, or actions. The Bible is a Book to be taught, not a memorial to be set up. The contents of the Bible is our teaching tool.

Just outside the Sunday school room in the hall is the secretaries' table. This is a reception center for the children coming in. New ones are registered. The class number assigned to all the children is also checked. This is the place where all attendance records are to be compiled. It is good to keep the business of the secretary center outside of the Sunday school room.

How Is the Preschool Department Staffed, and What Are the Duties of the Staff?

Let's begin with the superintendent. The superintendent is the person who oversees the Sunday school department. She is, of course, answerable to the pastor for program plans and for teaching. The pastor is, of course, directly responsible to the Lord for every detail of the operation of the church. In addition to the Sunday school lesson, the superintendent plans what other teachings she would like to see in the department. She plans with the teachers the Spring and Fall Programs and any other special times. She plans the Sunday morning program. It is a good thing for one person to be the housekeeper for the department, one who files visual aids and who keeps things stored, neat, and ready for use the next time. The superintendent is a good person to be the housekeeper for the department. The superintendent also ought to look upon her teachers as though they are her Sunday school class. She is their leader. She is their teacher. She is just as concerned about each of them individually as the teacher is concerned about each individual pupil. The final decisions about anything in the department depend upon the superintendent to lead the department, so the superintendent depends upon the teachers to build all the classes. There is a closeness of fellowship between the superintendent and the teachers of the department. We all have one common goal. That goal is to teach boys and girls the Bible and to love Jesus. When we are together in our teachers' meetings, we are all on a first-name basis with each other. However, when we come together on Sunday morning to work in the department with the children, we are quite formal with each other so that the children will be encouraged to show respect for us. For instance, we do not use last names for the teachers in our department. The last names are a bit difficult for the children. We use first names preceded with the word "Miss." I am "Miss Erma." Some of my teachers are "Miss Marie," "Miss Dorothy," "Miss Eilene," "Miss Leona," etc. When we come on Sunday morning, we are careful not to carry on individual, personal conversations with each other. We try to confine our conversation with each other to the actual business at hand. When we address each other, we address each other as "Miss Marie," etc.

Under the Lord's leadership a certain kind of personality of teacher has come to the preschool department. This kind of teacher has complete command of children. She sees the need for firm discipline without impatience and without temper. She sees the need for true love for them. She has a rather quiet, not too aggressive, personality to work with preschool children. Because the departments grow, because new children are constantly coming — some frightened, some too noisy, some hard to handle — the teacher of the preschool child has to be flexible to change. She loves the children and she shows it. She tries not to tattle on the children. She tries not to take discipline problems from the Sunday school department back to the parents. She is also careful not to gossip about the child. She might, however, bring up the problem at the departmental teachers' meeting in order to get advice from co-workers.

Every child is born a sinner and every child is going to misbehave some time or another. If there is a constant problem with the child, this problem indicates a need. Instead of becoming fed up or impatient or disgusted with a child who indicates a need, the teacher of the preschool child should be concerned. By praying for a child, by showing him that the teacher loves him, and by visiting him in his home and perhaps taking him a small gift and showing a little extra special attention, discipline problems can be overcome. If the teacher tattles to a parent about a child, this either puts the parent on the defensive because he doesn't want anyone to think ill of his child, or it makes the parent discipline or punish the child for bad behavior long after the bad behavior is completed and has been forgotten by the child.

Ernie was a brilliant little boy, far more brilliant than the other little boys and girls in his room. Because things went a little bit slowly for him in Sunday school in order that the other boys and girls might be reached, Ernie reacted with bad behavior. When the teacher caught on to the fact that Ernie was such a brilliant little boy, she started to find special little memory verses for him to learn and to repeat to her the next Sunday. She started giving him extra little jobs that he could do to help out until Sunday school started or as Sunday school was ending. This solved Ernie's behavior problem.

Timmy came to Sunday school the first Sunday kicking, screaming, and throwing a regular tantrum when his mother tried to leave him at the Sunday school door. The superintendent suggested to the mother that she leave and that she was sure that Timmy would be all right. Timmy kicked the superintendent and insisted that he was not going to come into the department. The superintendent almost bodily dragged him into the room, firmly sat him down in a chair, and said, "Timmy, until you can behave properly you will sit here alone; you may not sit with the other boys and girls. We love you and we are glad you are here in Sunday school, but you must be quiet now." She insisted that Timmy stay in the chair, and she watched to see that her orders were carried out. She gave him a paper, but the rest of the morning Timmy sat alone on that chair. That afternoon the superintendent began thinking about Timmy and wondered if she had handled his problem properly. She prayed much for Timmy that day and all the rest of the week hoping that Timmy would come back to Sunday school and that he would learn to love it so that he might be reached with the Bible teaching too. The next Sunday, much to the superintendent's delight, here came Timmy. He greeted the superintendent with a smile and said, "Here, I want you to have this." The superintendent took from his hand an old valentine that his daddy had given his mother. This seemed to be Timmy's way of saying, "I like you and I want to be a good boy and I want to show you that I do." Timmy and the superintendent have been fast friends ever since even though Timmy now is of junior age. The Lord knows the thoughts and needs of children, and He knows how to direct the superintendent and teachers even though they don't understand that particular child's problem. Without formal education in psychology and without the aid of a psychiatrist the Sunday school teacher can properly handle every problem that comes because the Holy Spirit understands all of these, and He directs.

How many children should one teacher handle? Who can really set a maximum number. If it becomes apparent, however, that a group is growing too large for the teacher to visit effectively and work effectively with the children, then the superintendent ought to suggest to the pastor or to the one who is enlisting new teachers for the department that another new teacher be added to the faculty of the department.

In addition to the superintendent and to the teachers of the department there is need for some good secretaries. Two secretaries should be seated at a reception desk to take down the names, addresses, telephone numbers, birthdays, and ages of the new children coming. The secretary marks the class number or the name of the teacher of the class to which the child is assigned. It is good to divide the class by areas so that the teacher in her visitation doesn't have to travel from one end of the town to the other to visit her absentees. After the new child is registered in the department it is good to have someone else take that child along with the duplicate of the slip that has been just filled out and introduce the child to his new teacher and to show him where he will sit every Sunday when he comes to the Sunday school. Unless it has been made clear by the person who brings the child to the department that this child is definitely only a one-time visitor, perhaps from a distant state, the secretary during the week makes up a class enrollment card for that child and inserts it with the other cards in his teacher's packet. This card has room on it for the name of the child, his address, his birthday, his age, his telephone number.   There are also squares on the card for checking his attendance every Sunday of the year.   Because the card is blank on the back, this affords a place for the teacher to make any kind of notation she desires about the child's home life — things that will be helpful to her in knowing the child and his needs and how to pray for him.   The cards in the teacher's packet are her property.

In addition to this card the secretary makes in duplicate a 3 x 5 card to go into a main file that contains the names and addresses of all the boys and girls who are enrolled in the department.   This file is helpful inasmuch as the class number and the name of the teacher to which the child is assigned is marked on the card. It is not necessary to keep an attendance record on this card, for this is just a master file.   We need to know the name of every child that is expected within the department.   Oftentimes the child comes and cannot remember in whose class he should sit.   We ask his name, go to the file that is in alphabetical order by last names, see the number of the class to which he has been assigned, then take the child and say, "This is the class where you sit."

It is necessary to work with these files weekly.   Sometimes the teacher in calling on the children realizes that an address has been incomplete or incorrect.   Upon learning correct and new information she tells the secretary so that the teacher's packet can always be up to date, the 3 x 5 card file is made correct, and the addressograph plate is changed.   The secretaries have this weekly responsibility. They also aid in sending out the mailings each time there is a mailing to go out.

In the church office letters are made up, mimeographed and folded.   Then the secretaries take these letters, address them by using the addressograph plates, sort them by zip code, count them, and tie them.   Then once again the letters are turned over to someone in the church office who actually takes them to the post office for mailing.

In addition to the two secretaries who are at the reception table, there is another secretary standing at the door whose primary purpose is to greet the children.   She is holding in her hand an offering receptacle.   As the child comes through the door he places his offering in the bank, basket, or whatever she is holding. She is a cheerful lady who also loves children and greets them with a smile and has a little word to say to them as they pass through the door going to their class.

As the department grows, the obtaining of an accurate head count becomes more difficult. So there is a fourth secretary standing just inside the door who pins a tag on each child who comes in. The tags have been prepared ahead of time by someone in the department. As far as the child knows, the tag is simply a picture or a pennant or something to represent the special program in which the department is involved. However, there is a number on the back of the tag, or the pennant, or whatever it is. The tags are consecutively numbered from one to however many children are expected in the department that Sunday. The number on the last tag used represents the number of teachers and children present that day.

How Are the Children Divided Into Classes, and How Do the Teachers and Pupils Become Acquainted With Each Other?

Brief reference has been made as to how the department is divided. More detail follows. Because these are preschool children the classes can be mixed — boys and girls in each class. Names of the children coming into the department are divided by the area in which they live. The superintendent and a co-worker evaluate the size classes by area. The boundaries are determined according to the number of pupils that come from the particular area. The secretaries are then informed where the boundaries are. For instance, a particular area for a particular teacher should go from such and such street on the north to such and such street on the south, from such and such street on the east to such and such street on the west. Of course, it is necessary to have a map to determine this. Then the teachers are informed of their areas.

In the department a table is a class. Because calling should be done two by two, two classes are put together. Two tables are set side by side or end to end. Two teachers work two classes together. This is called a class group.

These teachers get to know the children from both classes and during the week they meet and do their calling together. One teacher might have an area in one end of town and her partner might have another area for calling. They determine where they should go that week to do their class visitation.

Because a little preschool child does not always remember where he sits when he comes to Sunday school, it is helpful to mark each class by some kind of picture. For instance, one class might be a class of lambs. The picture of a lamb is painted on the back of his chair. The teacher wears a tag that is a picture of this lamb. She might send the same tag to the pupil in the mail. At Promotion Day especially he wears this tag to Sunday school himself. The teacher, the pupil, and the chairs all match each other. This way the child knows where he goes until he gets acquainted with his teacher and remembers where his class is in the room.

It is very important that the teacher will get into the home of each pupil just as soon as possible after the pupil is new in her class. The pupil needs to get to know the teacher. The teacher needs to get to know the pupil. Interest in the child is an excellent way to get the foot in the door for the need of witnessing to the parents and other members of the family also.

How Is the Department Operated on Sunday Morning?

All teachers and superintendents should arrive early enough to greet the first children who come. Our Sunday school starts at 9:40. Ten minutes after nine is not too early for a superintendent and a secretary and at least one or two teachers to be there. The other teachers ought to be arriving soon thereafter.

Sometime during the week the superintendent has made a check on the room to be sure that it is set up properly for the following Sunday. Everything that is needed in the way of visual aids, music, etc., are set out by the superintendent at that time. She is sure that the tables and the chairs are in order and that the room is exactly the way she wants it for the next Sunday.

As the pupils come to the preschool department they are

greeted cheerfully, each one being made to feel as if he has been expected and as if the teachers and the superintendent are thrilled to see him. If they are not sincere in this greeting, the child senses this. The pupil goes directly to his class table. If it is a day that he is wearing a coat and hat, he puts his hat with his coat and puts his coat on the back of his chair or the coat could be hung on a hook in the room or a place in the hall. The teacher is at the table expecting the pupil. She talks to him as he comes and lets him talk to her, showing her his new shoes, his sore finger, telling her about the new baby brother or sister in his home, telling her that Daddy has come to Sunday school today, etc. She will listen to everything as if it is the most important news of the day. At the same time she is checking the attendance. She is marking on the card for each individual pupil the fact that the child is present today.

Because some children have arrived so early, the superintendent has started what she calls the "Early Bird Club." She has the children who arrive so early to come to the story rug after they have been to their table. On the story rug the children are sitting participating in the finger plays that the superintendent is leading, learning new Scripture passages and repeating them with the superintendent. About ten minutes before it is actually time for the department to start Sunday school, the superintendent sends the children back to their tables. This way the teacher makes sure that she did not miss any child in her original attendance check.

Now it is time for Sunday school to begin. The superintendent has a hand bell. It is a pretty sounding bell which she rings. When the children hear the bell ring, they all come to the story rug. If the department has grown very large and the teachers are quite busy taking attendance because of so many children coming in at the same time, the superintendent might have a public address system. She just picks up the microphone and says, "Teachers, whenever you are ready, send your children, please, to the story rug. It is time for us to start Sunday school." The piano player sitting at the piano now is playing some little tunes while we are waiting for everybody to get assembled on the story rug.

The pianist begins playing the opening song. We might

sing together, "Our Sunday school has begun. Our Sunday school has begun. We will ask our heavenly Father, please, to bless us every one." Then we all want to pray together. We say our little prayer verse: "My feet are very, very still. My hands I fold this way. I bow my head and close my eyes as quietly I pray." Everyone gets very, very quiet, and the superintendent leads the department in a short prayer asking God's guidance for the day, thanking Him that so many boys and girls have come to Sunday school, and asking Jesus that they might come to love Jesus, because Jesus loves them. Some Sundays children come to the superintendent and say, "Teacher, would you pray for my daddy? He is sick." A child once said, "Teacher, my cousin was hit by a car this week and got killed. Would you pray for his family?" The superintendent has learned not to ask for prayer requests, but because the children realize that she will honor the request, they come to her individually with something that is on their heart and ask her to pray for them. The superintendent also tries to remember to pray for any teacher who might be sick that day or have an illness or bereavement in the family so the children will learn to pray for everything and to be concerned about everyone else also.

Then it is time to sing. Singing the same songs Sunday after Sunday for a certain period of time helps the children to learn the songs. It also gets the song in their hearts and in their minds so that during the week they remember to sing the songs. The songs should be sung as slowly as they need to be for that age child to pronounce the words correctly, to know what he is singing, and to follow along so that everyone is singing together with understanding. In singing songs as well as in teaching, the ability of a child to understand and the progress he is making in growth and understanding should be taken into consideration. For instance, by the time the child is in kindergarten he is singing longer songs than the child in the Nursery Department. He is also singing songs with many different words in them. He is also learning to write his name and to spell his name. So we sing a little song that says, "I can spell a lovely name, J-E-S-U-S." We are holding up five fingers, pointing to a different finger as we say a different letter. All preschool children love "Jesus Loves Me." This is the basis of their singing. Preschool children should be learning to sing such songs as, "Trust and Obey," "Oh, How I Love Jesus" "Praise Him, Praise Him," "Who Can Make a Flower? I'm Sure I Can't, Can You?" "Jesus Wants Me for a Sunbeam," "Oh, Be Careful," and little songs about Bible characters.

After we have sung two or three songs, it is time for the Bible story. To have a Bible story early in the Sunday morning program is very important with little children. We need to teach them while they are still fresh before they get too tired to listen. We insist that they sit quietly and hear the teacher who is telling the story. Since the department is all together for the entire Sunday school time, the teachers take turns telling the Bible stories. A schedule could be drawn up so that the teacher can anticipate when it will be her turn to tell the Bible story. All of the teachers have been taught the Bible story on Wednesday evening by the superintendent, but just one teacher actually prepares thoroughly to teach the lesson. However, they should all know the story and be prepared to answer any questions the child has. It is also a good idea for another teacher besides the one assigned the story to be ready to tell it, for there might be sickness or some other reason why at the last minute she cannot be present on Sunday morning.

At the beginning of Bible story time, the superintendent says, "Children, this is the most important time of Sunday school. Everyone's hands are kept to himself. Everyone's eyes are looking this way, and everyone's lips are closed tight. We are not going to say anything unless our teacher tells us to say something. Today it is Miss Leona's turn to tell the Bible story. As she comes we will say, 'Good morning, Miss Leona,' and then we will not say anything unless she asks us to. Come now, Miss Leona. 'GOOD MORNING, MISS LEONA.'"

Then the Bible story is taught. The teacher has her Bible in her hand and before she lays it down in order to tell the story she tells the children, "This story that I am going to tell you today is from the Bible. If it is from the Bible, it is a true story. It really happened." The teacher must be well prepared before she teaches the little children. She must *not* read any of the story. The teacher needs to forget that there are other teachers listening to her. She is there to tell the children the story. She puts herself completely into it. On Wednesday night at the teachers' meeting the methods to be used in telling the story have been discussed. If there are objects to be used in telling the story, they have been completely prepared. If flannelgraph is going to be used, it is in order so that the first figure to be used is on top, etc. The flannelboard is there for use before Sunday school begins. If the chalkboard is to be used, it is in its place. If the teacher is going to use children to help dramatize the story as she tells it, she is sure that there is space enough at the front of the room to move around.

The teacher comes prepared to use language that the children can understand. If there is a new word that she wishes to teach the children that day, she has well thought out conversation, objects, or actions that she can use to teach the children that word. For example, "Joseph's brother threw Joseph into a *pit.* What is a pit? A pit is a great big hole in the ground. How big is this great big hole in the ground? If someone were down in this pit, he couldn't climb up." If any part of the Bible story utilizes words that are unfamiliar to the children, the teacher just can count on the fact that she will lose the attention of the children who do not understand.

Whatever Sunday school literature the teacher uses, the teacher is to remember that that literature is her tool and not her master. She is to take it and carefully consider it in prayer. Does it really teach what the Bible teaches? Does it teach what the children need to know? Does it teach what the children need in their lives? If it does not, then the teacher must alter the lesson to make it what it ought to be.

After telling the Bible story the teacher teaches the children a memory verse. In the Nursery Department the children can learn a verse of about three or four words; therefore, only a part of a Bible verse that is applicable to the story can be learned. In the Beginner Department whole sentences of Bible verses should be memorized.

After the teaching of the Bible verse the superintendent or the songleader can lead the boys and girls in the singing of a song.   Perhaps a new song will be learned.   This is a good time to introduce the new song.   How is the new song introduced?   The superintendent sings it alone to the children.   "Children, I am going to sing you a new song today."   That is all the time that is given to that song for that Sunday.   The next Sunday she might say, "Some of you will remember the song that I am going to sing today. If you remember it, you help me sing it."   Then the next Sunday she will say, "I know a lot of you boys and girls know this song that we are going to sing today."   The song becomes theirs, and it can be used eventually at the beginning of the Sunday school hour before the Bible story is told.

Now the children are tired and need to move around a little.   It is not absolutely necessary now that they all remain so still that we can hear a pin drop, so this is a good time in the program to welcome new boys and girls — and new boys and girls need to be welcomed.   Here the superintendent depends very largely upon the teachers to help the new boys and girls to stand up.   The superintendent can say, "Who is new today?"   Some boys and girls do not realize that they are new, and some boys and girls who have been there two or three Sundays already think they are still new.   So the teachers need to say, "This little boy is new today," or "This little girl is new today," and help them to stand up.   The superintendent then says, "We are so happy to have you all here today.   We would like to learn your names.   What is your name?"   She hears the first name of the child, and everybody then says, "Hi, Sandra," or "Hi, Tommy."   A welcome button is pinned on each new child there that day.   Then a welcome song is sung to the entire group of the new children by the children who have already been in Sunday school.   "Welcome, welcome to our Sunday school.   Jesus loves you and we are glad you are here.   Please come back next Sunday. We will look for you.   You are welcome here in Sunday school."   The little boys and girls sit back down on the story rug.

Now it is time for birthdays.   "Teachers, who has had a birthday since last Sunday?"   Don't ask the boys and girls.   Everybody has had a birthday some time or other, and they would all like to be honored. The teachers need to come to Sunday school each Sunday prepared to tell the superintendent who in their classes had a birthday since last Sunday. The birthday children come to the front of the room. The superintendent carefully explains to the birthday children that the cake we are using today is a make-believe cake. We do not use a real cake in Sunday school for birthday time because we couldn't use it every Sunday if we did. Unless this is explained every Sunday, this make-believe cake (which looks so real) will make birthday time a real disappointment to the children who think you really have cake to pass out. If only one or two children come at birthday time, each child could be honored separately. If, however, the department is large enough that there are five or six or more children who have had birthdays that week, the children need to be honored as a group so as not to take up too much time. If the children are honored separately, as many candles as the child is old are placed on the birthday cake. If the children are honored as a group, there is a candle on the cake for each child. Some children have brought their birthday pennies with them. The pennies are dropped one by one into the slot of the artificial birthday cake. We say, "Jesus loved Tommy one year; Jesus loved Tommy two years; Jesus loved Tommy three years, etc.," for each child who drops his birthday pennies into the birthday cake. What if a child brings a nickel instead of five pennies when he is five years old? We carefully explain to the children that the nickel is the same as five pennies, and so Jesus loved Tommy five years. The candles then are lit on the birthday cake. We are very careful at this time to teach the children caution about fire. Only the superintendent lights the candles on the cake and the children stand back so as to be very, very careful not to get burned. While the candles are lit, the other boys and girls sing "Happy Birthday" to the birthday children. Then the children count, "One, two, three, blow," and the birthday children blow out their candles.

The department then has a little inexpensive picture to hand to each birthday child. We prefer to use the picture of Jesus and the sheep as a gift from the Beginner Department.   As we hand the picture to the child we say, "Happy birthday from the Beginner Department.   You may take this picture home.   It is yours to keep.   You may hang it on the wall or put it on your dresser."

Now it is time to talk about the offering that we have put into the offering basket or the bank at the door.   We take a container that has been emptied (by this time the money has been taken to the Sunday school office.)   We choose a child to come up to the front and hold this empty container, and then we say, "When we brought our offering this morning, did I (the superintendent pointing to herself) get that money?   Oh, no.   Did they (pointing to the teachers) get that money?   Oh, no.   Why do we bring our offering to Sunday school?   We bring it that more boys and girls will get to know about Jesus.   We use it to buy chairs, etc., (pointing to one or two items on different Sundays that have been purchased with the money that we bring to Sunday school)."   Then the child who is holding the receptacle bows his head and he prays out loud thanking Jesus for the offering.   The superintendent will say to the child, "Do you want to pray by yourself, or shall I help you with the words?"   The majority of the children will say, "I would like for you to help me with the words."

So the superintendent says to the child in the child's ear very softly, "Dear Heavenly Father. . ."

The child repeats, "Dear Heavenly Father. . ."

". . . Thank you that we can bring our offering."

The child repeats, "Thank you that we can bring our offering."

". . . use it to tell other boys and girls. . ."

". . . use it to tell other boys and girls. . ."

". . . about Jesus."

". . . about Jesus."

". . . In Jesus' name we pray.   Amen."

". . . In Jesus' name we pray.   Amen."

Then the empty receptacle is handed back to the secretary and the child goes back and sits on the story rug.

Now all of the children need to stand to their feet and relax.   We might just stand and stretch and see how tall we can be or how high we can reach.   We might sing a song while we are standing and relaxing from sitting for so long a time. We might repeat together some memory passages that we have learned from the Bible. We need to remember that these are little children and that little children's attention span is not as long as that of adults, nor are little children capable of staying in one place as long as adults.

After the relaxation time the superintendent says, "Everyone sit down now." With much enthusiasm she introduces the next item on the program. This is a good time for a conduct story, but she can't just say at this point, "I want to tell you a story." If she uses this method of approach to the children at this time in the morning procedure, she won't get the children's attention. If she is using flannelgraph figures, she should start out immediately to put a figure on the board and begin speaking with an action sentence or two about that figure. The children will be "with her" if she does it well.

Perhaps the teacher has chosen to teach a conduct lesson with the story with the use of puppets. It is good to give some thought to having a puppet stage in a preschool department, especially as the child reaches four and five years old. The stage need not be anything more elaborate than three boards hinged together behind which the teacher or the superintendent who handles the puppets hide. The middle wooden board needs to have a window in it with a curtain over it. The window needs to be the same height as the teacher's head. She is hiding behind the curtain and her hands are up in front of the curtain operating the puppets. The puppets could teach such things as: It is not nice to stick out your tongue. You could have a puppet who is an owl and name him Mr. Wise. Mr. Wise tells the children about a friend that he is going to introduce to them that day. Up comes his friend and it is a green frog. Mr. Wise says, "Green, how are you today?" (However, Mr. Wise tries to talk in a real deep voice.)

Greeny just makes a sort of croaking sound as frogs do. Then Mr. Wise says, "Greeny, I saw you stick your tongue way, way out and then draw it back in the other day. Greeny, why did you do this?"

Greeny just croaks. Then Mr. Wise says, "Oh, you do this to catch the food that you are going to eat. A fly landed on your tongue and you brought it back in and you ate that fly. That was your supper."

Greeny croaks in agreement. Then Mr. Wise says to the children, "Frogs stick out their tongues so that they can eat, but boys and girls don't need to stick out their tongues to eat. In fact, boys and girls should never stick out their tongues, should they?" The children will agree with him that this should not be done. This ends the puppet show for the day with Mr. Wise and Greeny saying good-bye to the children and promising to come back another time.

Before the teacher who is operating the puppet steps behind the puppet stage, she could say to another teacher, "I am going into the woods to see if I can find Mr. Wise. Would you stay here with the children and see that they are all right until I get back? That teacher comes to the front of the room and talks to the children about what they might possibly see. This way they are kept in perfect order until the time for the puppet show to start.

Mr. Wise on another day might introduce Silly Willy to the boys and girls. Silly Willy is a wolf who really does act silly and gets awfully wild in front of the children. Mr. Wise talks to Silly Willy about the fact that there are times when it is good to run, play, be loud and noisy, and laugh, but there are also times when we need to be quiet. We don't run in the church building any more than we run in our homes. We can run outside though, and we can run in the basement of our house. Puppets can teach the children many conduct lessons much more effectively than we can by scolding and nagging at the children.

After the conduct story the superintendent might want to make some promotional announcement about next Sunday's program and how every boy and girl ought to be there and bring their friends, too. A big aid in making announcements has been a toy mouse. (The toy mouse was used two or three Sundays. Then the superintendent decided she didn't need to use him any more but that she could use something else in making announcements. The Sunday she did not use him many children said, "Where is Mr. Church Mouse? We would like to see Mr. Church Mouse." Since that Sunday he has been used almost every Sunday to make announcements about what is going to happen next Sunday in Sunday school.) The children just love Mr. Church Mouse. He stays in a shoe box because a mouse can make his home any place. This shoe box stays on the closet shelf. Because Mr. Church Mouse is in the church building all week long, he sees and knows all that is going to happen there. Sometimes before talking with Mr. Church Mouse the teacher can pretend that she hears a noise. She goes closer and closer to the shoe box where the church mouse is. She picks up the box, listens, and says, "Yes, I think that noise is coming from this box." She opens the box and tells the boys and girls that there is something in there that they ought to see. Of course, after he has been used two or three times the children will guess that it is Mr. Church Mouse.

"Do you think he is asleep today or awake?" We discuss what he is doing and what he has been doing. Then we take him out of the shoe box for the children to see. Because he is so cute you can just look around at the children and they are fascinated with him without any conversation for a few seconds. Then the superintendent can talk with the church mouse and ask him what special news he has for the children today. The church mouse then whispers into the superintendent's ear, and the superintendent tells the children what the church mouse wants them to know. Because the children like to pretend so much, the superintendent pretends, too.

Now it is almost time to dismiss Sunday school. The children are sent back to their tables a group at a time. They are cautioned repeatedly to go very carefully and to go very quietly so as not to bump into somebody or to step on somebody. They are instructed to sit down on their chairs at the tables. The teachers stay at the tables while the children are being called for by their parents. The people who come for the children stand outside the door of the room giving the name of the child for whom they are calling. This is a time when a public address system is most helpful. A secretary at the door calls out the name of a child. The teacher at the table recognizes the name of that child and sees to it that the child goes to the door to meet his parents or whoever is calling for him. No child is ever allowed to leave the room alone. Either the parents or another adult relative must call for the child. In the case of a child who has come to Sunday school on a church bus, the bus captain must come for him. Of course, bus children do not leave until the church service is over so they stay for the Story Hour taught in the same room during the church service. The Sunday school teachers stay with their classes until the Story Hour workers come in to take their places.

What Do We Do During Special Promotional Times?

For ten to twelve weeks each spring and fall our Sunday school puts on a special effort to reach new people. We work to grow during these periods so that more homes and more lives might be reached with the Gospel. Each department is instructed by the pastor to lay down special plans for this promotional time and then to present these plans to him.

The program is geared to the understanding, interests, and needs of the boys and girls. For instance, we might choose a theme of Christian traffic laws. To encourage the boys and girls to bring their friends to Sunday school, each Sunday they bring somebody they can come to the front of the room and put on a policeman hat. The child who has brought the most boys and girls that Sunday is taken out into the hall or to another room and dressed in a policeman outfit. He is especially honored because he brought the most visitors that Sunday. Then these children who have brought visitors to Sunday school stand in front of the room with their policeman hats and the policeman uniform on the one child. They shake their fingers at all of the children in the room, and they say all together, "We must do right."

This simple time of recognition is loved by the children, and they work hard to wear the policeman hat or to wear the entire policeman costume. We sing songs appropriate to this theme. One Sunday a man who is a Christian policeman and a member of our church comes into our department in his policeman's uniform — including the gun. The superintendent interviews this Christian policeman. The children learn that the policeman is their friend and that he is there to help them to obey the laws as well as to help them if they are lost, etc. The policeman explains to the children that the gun is not to be used by anybody but him and that he doesn't want to use it unless he really has to. In explaining the gun, he doesn't lift it from his holster. He explains to the children each part of his uniform—the badge, the cap, etc. Then he tells the boys and girls his Christian testimony. He tells that he trusts Jesus and wants to please Him in everything that he is doing.

Another Sunday a Christian magician comes in and does some tricks that have an object lesson about Christian living or about salvation.

We might have a special party time one Sunday when we have ice cream, or we might have cupcakes one Sunday. Before we eat we bow our heads, of course, and thank Jesus for the refreshments. This is teaching the children to pray before they eat at home.

From companies that sell inexpensive notions we order toys and gifts that the children can take home with them. We are allowed a maximum amount of money to spend through the Sunday school funds, and we are to budget our expenditures for our special spring or fall program within this allowance.

One Sunday everyone gets a policeman's badge to wear and take home. Another Sunday each child receives and wears a mouse pin that reminds him of Mr. Church Mouse. Another Sunday he will receive an inexpensive New Testament to take home with him. Whatever gifts the children take home from the preschool departments, there is some sort of appropriate meaning in connection with the theme for that time of the year. All children receive that gift and all children receive the same gift on the particular Sunday.

Another special promotional theme could be Christian soldiers. Plastic soldiers that look like English guards can be purchased and put on the wall in the front of the room. If a child brings a visitor to Sunday school, he is permitted to march in the Christian soldiers' parade. He is allowed to choose a rhythm instrument to play. These children march around the room playing their instruments while the pianist plays "Onward, Christian Soldiers." Just to give special honor, or special recognition, or a special activity to the child that brings someone to Sunday school at this age is enough, and is better with this age child than giving him a gift for bringing visitors to Sunday school. The child understands that the visitors that he brings must be those who come into his department with him, so the superintendent and teachers can see that these visitors have actually come.   Here again the teachers help the superintendent to know which children have actually brought visitors with them and be sure that the children who deserve recognition get it.

Of course, we seek to reach attendance goals during these special promotional times.   Each number that the department turns in represents a pupil who has attended for that day.   This pupil represents a home and represents people who need Jesus or people who need a church home.

Do We Teach Special Scripture Passages in the Beginner Department?

Yes, we do.   The sooner a child starts to memorize Scriptures and Scripture passages, the more he will know the Bible when he reaches adulthood.   The twenty-third Psalm can be taught to beginners.   It is taught over a period of perhaps six months.   It is taught a phrase at a time, using stories to illustrate each phrase. It is taught using motions. The children start by standing straight with their hands at their sides saying, "Psalm 23. (Pointing upward they say), *The Lord* (pointing to themselves they say) *is my shepherd:* (With their hands back down at their sides they say shaking their heads), *I shall not want.* (Putting their hands together and leaning their faces on their hands they say), *He maketh me to lie down in green pastures.* (Straightening up and reaching up with a hand as if they were putting it into someone else's hand), *He leadeth me beside the still waters.* (Clapping their hands rapidly they say), *He restoreth my soul.* (Reaching out their hand as if they are clasping another's hand again they say), *He leadeth me in the* (and then with their two hands held parallel they gesture straight out in front of them), *paths of righteousness...* (and pointing upward they say), *for His name's sake.* (Then bowing their heads and covering their heads with their arms they say), *Yea, though I walk through the valley of the shadow of death...* (And straightening up with their arms back down at their sides and smiles on their faces they say), *I will fear no evil: for thou art with me.* (And then as if clasping a rod in one hand they say), *thy rod* (as if they were clasping a staff in the other hand), *and thy staff they comfort me.* (As if they were straightening a tablecloth on a table, they say), *Thou preparest a table before me...* (they are clasping their hands together in front of them)... *in the presence of mine enemies:...* (as if they were pouring a bottle of oil over their head they say), *...thou anointest my head with oil;* (moving their hands in circular motion over and over each other they say), *my cup runneth over.* (Holding up the index finger with one hand they say), *Surely goodness* (holding up the index finger of the other hand they say), *and mercy shall follow me all the days of my life:* (They clasp their hands together in front of them and then stoop as if they are sitting down while they say), *and I will dwell in the house of the Lord for ever."*

Before and during the Easter season we learn Romans 3:23, Romans 6:23, and John 3:16 over a period of a few Sundays. On Easter Sunday we send home with the children a little Easter basket that the teachers have made out of construction paper. In the basket is a handful of Easter basket grass. Nestled in the grass are some jelly beans and a chocolate cross. We talk with the children about the significance of the colors of the jelly beans, using the "Wordless Book Chorus" colors.

We also teach at least the first three verses of Psalm 100 in the Beginner Department. While the passages are being taught conduct stories are told to illustrate the meaning of them. Children who know what we have learned thus far are permitted to come to the front of the room and to say it to the other children or to lead the other children as they all say it.

A promotional letter into the home includes the fact to the parents that we are memorizing a certain Scripture passage. Some parents will thus set aside time to help the child in the home in the memorization of these passages. As with the Bible story the children understand from where these passages come. They are coming from God's Word—the Bible.

Special effort and attention are given to explain the spiritual significance of the important holidays of our year. We want the children to understand especially the meaning of Thanksgiving, Christmas, and Easter. At times like Memorial Day and the Fourth of July we want them to learn a special pride in our country. For Mother's Day and Father's Day it is good to teach the children that they should obey Mother and Daddy and that they should show their love for them. Many times we make special gifts for them to take home to Mother and Daddy on Mother's Day and Father's Day.

What Kind of Parties Can We Have for Our Department?

Children love parties! Preschool children love them just as much as school-age children. At Halloween time everybody is having a party, but we do not have Halloween parties for preschool children. The masks and the costumes destroy so much of the identity of the children for each other that it is frightening to them. The entire party time would no doubt be spent drying tears and trying to comfort the children if they had on masks and costumes before they are old enough to fully appreciate the Halloween party. So while everyone else in the Sunday school is having a Halloween party, we have a circus party. As the children come to the Beginner Department they hear circus music playing on a phonograph. They are greeted at the door by a teacher who hands them a bag of popcorn. They sit down in a chair, eat their popcorn, listen to the music, and look around at the special circus decorations while they are waiting for everybody to come and for the party to begin. There is a clown present who does some tricks for the boys and girls and makes them laugh. Then there is an animal trainer who comes. The animal trainer is a teacher who has made some cages from some boxes. She has cut slits in the boxes to make them look like bars and has painted the boxes brown. These are the cages for the stuffed animals that the teachers have contributed for the use of the animal trainer for that day. The animal trainer takes the stuffed animals one at a time and pretends to do tricks with them. The children clap and have a big time. The party includes time for a story—a story with a special Christian emphasis. Perhaps the story is about the boys and girls inviting somebody else to come to Sunday school the next day with them. Then there are refreshments around the table. The children are led (a few at a time) to the tables so that they do not bump each other around the tables. The table has been set by some teachers who have not been busy with other responsibilities during the party. Big animal cookies that are frosted and a simple punch drink are served. This light refreshment is thoroughly enjoyed by the children by now for they are thirsty, but not very hungry.

Now it is almost time for the party to end. It lasted for one and one-half hours. It is time for the people to start coming for their children. They will come one at a time, however, so we need to do something to keep the children busy while others are being called for at the door. We begin to play simple games. When the children are called for at the door, they just leave the game and go home. The others continue playing until their name is called also. We play "Follow the Leader" and do things to imitate different animals. We play "Ring Around the Rosy" or "Farmer in the Dell." We try not to make the party too strict, nor too complicated, for we like the children to laugh and have a thoroughly good time at our party. We want them to see that the teachers and superintendent can laugh and have some fun with the children.

We have a Christmas party. As the children arrive at the Christmas party they are each given an ornament to hang on the Christmas tree. Of course, they are given very careful guidance by one of the teachers as they hang their ornaments on the tree. Some Christmas carols are playing on the phonograph for the Christmas party. The children sit down and they start to sing with the person who is leading the singing of Christmas songs which they can sing. While the children sit in a circle, one of the teachers reads a special Christmas story to the boys and girls. After simple refreshments the children play games again such as "Toy Shop," and as they leave they receive a peppermint cane to take home.

Throughout the year individual classes have parties also. In the summertime the teachers take their classes to the park where they just swing, serve some refreshments, and take them home.   Some teachers take their classes to the zoo. These kinds of parties are best conducted on the individual class basis, or two classes join together so that two teachers can handle the group—asking for help from mothers and other volunteers.

Do We Do Any Handwork During Sunday School Time?

No, there is not time to do any handwork in that period. The handwork is saved for the Story Hour after Sunday school is ended.   The children who do not stay for Story Hour receive the unfinished handwork at the door so that they might take it home where someone can help them work on it.

Why Do We Work So Hard on the Planning and Conducting of Our Preschool Sunday School Departments?

It is because it is the Lord's business and we are answerable to Him to do the very best job we can do in order to influence the entire lives of boys and girls for Christ.   We want the children to like Sunday school so that they will continue to come to learn the Word of God and to learn to trust Jesus some day as their personal Saviour.

14. The Primary Department

(Written by Mrs. Johnny Colsten, Director of Primary Work at the First Baptist Church, Hammond, Indiana)

At the time of this writing we have two primary departments in the First Baptist Church of Hammond, Indiana. We have a separate department for all boys and girls in the first grade and another for those in the second grade. I have the privilege and responsibility of being the superintendent of the Primary I Department, which consists of first-grade boys and girls. On Promotion Day at the close of the Spring Program each year every boy and girl in our Sunday school who has completed kindergarten and is being promoted to first grade in public school is promoted to Primary I. He is assigned to my department. All boys and girls whom I have had the past year who are being promoted to second grade in the public schools are assigned to Primary II Department. After the first Sunday in the new department, each department may get their visitors and prospects from three grade levels — the grade level of the department, one grade level below, and one grade level above. Consequently, during the course of the year, Primary I Department consists mainly of first graders, but also has boys and girls in kindergarten and in second grade.

BEGINNING A SUNDAY SCHOOL YEAR

1. *Send a congratulatory card home with each graduating kindergarten child on Promotion Day.* In our Sunday school the department for the kindergarten children is called Begin-

ner II.   On Promotion Day I give their superintendent a supply of congratulatory cards from me.   The purpose of this card is not only to congratulate the child who is going to enter school, but also to inform him of the location of his new department.   An example of the card we give to the incoming first graders is shown below.

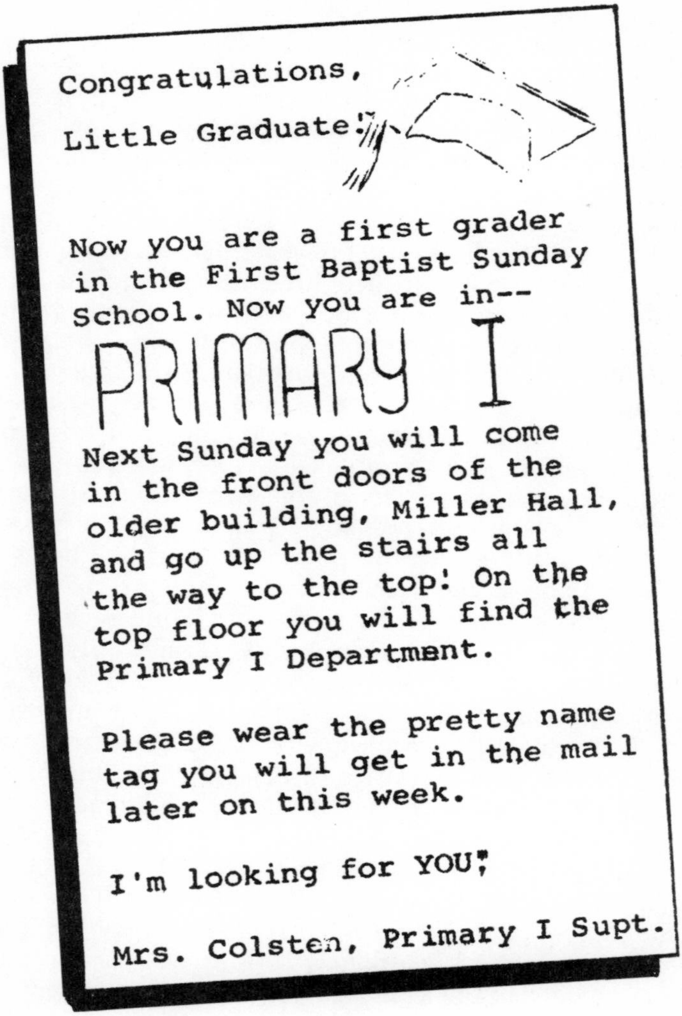

Congratulations,

Little Graduate!

Now you are a first grader in the First Baptist Sunday School. Now you are in--

PRIMARY I

Next Sunday you will come in the front doors of the older building, Miller Hall, and go up the stairs all the way to the top! On the top floor you will find the Primary I Department.

Please wear the pretty name tag you will get in the mail later on this week.

I'm looking for YOU!

Mrs. Colsten, Primary I Supt.

2. *The Primary I superintendent should make a brief visit to the Beginner II Department on Promotion Day.* Each year I arrange with the Beginner II superintendent to make this brief visit. She introduces me to the boys and girls as their new superintendent. I welcome them to Primary I and also remind them of the location of Primary I so they will know without a shadow of a doubt where to come the next Sunday. This visit to the Beginner II Department by the Primary I superintendent is of great benefit in giving the children the confidence that they will see someone they know when they come to the new department the following Sunday. Of course, this is advisable for every age department, but particularly so with the very young boys and girls.

3. *The new first graders should receive a welcome letter early in the week following Promotion Day.* This will help the boys and girls to be reminded of the name and location of their new department. It will also serve as good public relations between the new department and the parents of the new boys and girls. After all, the children have been comfortably situated in a department for one entire year. Making changes is never easy for young children. Every effort should be made to make the transition a happy one. The welcome letter sent this year to the boys and girls coming to Primary I Department is shown below.

(Illustration on next page)

Welcome!

to PRIMARY I

Dear Little Friend,

You are now a first grader in the First Baptist Sunday School. We are so happy you are now in the Primary I Department. All the teachers join me in saying, "Welcome!"

In Primary I we all meet together in our big room for an "opening assembly." Then we divide into thirteen classes. Each class of boys has a fine Christian gentleman for a teacher. Each class of girls has a lovely Christian lady for a teacher. You will love your teacher and class.

In a few days I will send you a name tag to wear when you come to Primary I this Sunday, June 2, 1968. When you get the name tag, keep it in a safe place until Sunday. Each class will have a different color for their name tags so all the children can find their classes more easily.

Your parents will be happy to know that I have been a a schoolteacher. Teaching first grade is my specialty. That means YOU, as a first grader, are very special to me. I'm looking for you this Sunday in Primary I.

Love,

Mrs. Colsten
Primary I Superintendent

Primary I - Top Floor - Miller Hall
First Baptist Church, 523 Sibley, Hammond, Indiana

4. *Later in the week following Promotion Day, each first grader should receive another letter with his personalized name tag enclosed.* Boys and girls need to see that they are wanted in a personal sort of way, not just as a mass of children. For this reason I have found it very helpful to use the personalized name tag each year at promotion time. There is another good reason for this. The individualized name tags greatly assist the new children in finding their new classes. You see, in Primary I the children are in small classes for the first time in their lives. Prior to this they have had large departmental teaching for the entire hour. This will be their first experience in a departmental setup — an opening assembly and divisions of small classes.

Some years I have used a particular theme such as animals, cowboy subjects, etc. This year I used simply different colors for the name tags. Most years I have used an object because all I wanted to put on the name tag was the child's name. However, this year, because of our new building, the boys and girls coming into my department have to enter a different building and go up three extra stories. Consequently, I felt it wise to print upon the name tag more than just the child's name. An example is shown below.

My name is _____ .

"I'm on my way to Primary I

On the top floor of Miller Hall.

You see, I'm now a first grader,

Growing very big and tall!"

The little poem on the name tag was a help to bus drivers and other adults who assisted boys and girls in coming to Sunday school and finding their new departments. If a child had difficulty finding Primary I and all his name tag said was his own name, then anyone who wanted to help him would not be able to assist him at all. This way anyone finding a child looking for Primary I could help him find the department because of the information on the tag.

5. *Coordinate the colors of the teacher's name tag, the teacher's chair, and the classroom doors with the color of the name tags of the children assigned to that particular class.* Currently we have thirteen classes in Primary I. This means that each class was assigned a different color. For example, let us take the color "red." The teacher wore a red name tag on the first Sunday the boys and girls came to Primary I. Each child who was assigned to that teacher was sent a red name tag. The teacher's chair had a red sign on the back of that chair. The classroom door was also labeled with a red sign. These signs are helpful for the entire year. Any boy or girl who comes the first Sunday, of course, is helped by the labeling of the chairs, classrooms, etc.; however, the class retains its color name throughout the entire year. This is helpful for children returning from vacation. They may not remember exactly where their class met, but they normally remember the color of their name tag or the sign on the classroom door, etc.

6. *On the first Sunday in the new department the superintendent should be certain that plenty of assistants are on hand early so that each new first grader can be personally greeted and assisted in meeting his new teacher.* No child should arrive in a new department and be left to find his place by himself. Each child should be warmly greeted. The assistant should greet the child that comes up the stairs with statements such as these: "Hi, there, Bobby. I am so glad that you are in Primary I. Let's see, you have an orange name tag. That means that you will be in Mr. Gifford's class. Come this way and I will take you to Mr. Gifford. I will show you where he sits and where his class of boys will sit. I will introduce him to you. My, you look fine this morning. Here he is. Mr. Gifford, this is Bobby Jones. Bobby, this is Mr. Gifford. He has an

orange name tag on just like yours."

The secretary or the assistant then leaves Bobby with Mr. Gifford and quickly goes back to the entrance of the department to greet another child.

7. *The opening assembly on that first Sunday in the new department should be very simple and clear.* New procedures must be explained, for as we have said, this is the first time these boys and girls have been in a departmental setup. The children before have had the security of entering one large room and staying altogether in that one room until the entire morning is completed. Now, things are different. The more simple and clear the procedure can be, the more confident the children will feel in their new location. This is vital! Many boys and girls are not encouraged by their parents to come to Sunday school. They come only if they are happy and comfortably situated.

The superintendent should lead the boys and girls in singing some songs with which they are familiar. She could teach them perhaps one new song, but no more on this first Sunday. In our case I taught the boys and girls our own welcome song and we sang it to ourselves. All the boys and girls were new in our department, and this way we could welcome ourselves to Primary I. This way we also learned our welcome song so that on the fifty-one succeeding Sundays we could welcome the boys and girls who would be new to our department.

Although the superintendent should be careful to make that first Sunday in Primary I interesting and exciting, she should never allow chaos to develop. Children should never feel that they have become free to misbehave in any way. Of course, a very well-planned opening assembly will prevent any such problems. Another prevention of problems is the simple stating of rules. Boys and girls who are going to be six years old are coming to a stage where they enjoy the feeling of belonging to a group with special rules. Organization has an appeal for them. So we call ourselves first graders immediately. Even though the boys and girls will not become first graders until September, throughout June, July, and August we refer to ourselves as first-grade boys and girls.

On the first Sunday in Primary I we practice saying the

name of our new department and the name of our new
superintendent. I tell the boys and girls, "Let's open the
windows and tell all the city of Hammond what department
we are." So we open a few windows a little higher than
they already were opened, and we put our hands around
our mouths. Very loudly we all say, "Primary I."

I reply, "Do you think they heard us three blocks up the
street or just one? Maybe they didn't hear us. Let's try
again."

This time they say, "PRIMARY I!"

Team spirit is important, and it must be developed from
the start so that boys and girls will have a sense of truly
belonging to the department.

8. *Dismiss the classes by the color of the name tag.* The
superintendent should close the opening assembly early
enough to allow time for orderly dismissal of classes. The
boys and girls should never be permitted to leave altogether.
The superintendent should observe that all are sitting very
straight and keeping their rows very neat. She should call
the name of the teacher and the name of the class color and
ask them to leave in a straight line and walk to their class
areas. She could say something like this: "Now we will
excuse the girls in Mrs. Springel's class. Mrs. Springel
and all of her girls have lavender name tags. The lavender
class may go now. Boys and girls, do you hear any sound?
I do not. They are not bumping their chairs. The girls
have not left their wraps or their purses or Bibles on their
chairs. They have taken everything with them. See how
nicely they are going to their class. That is wonderful,
isn't it?" With statements such as those the superintendent is
likewise encouraging everyone else to be just as neat and
just as careful about leaving the departmental assembly
room. Also, every boy and girl in that class is being reminded again of their class color and their teacher's name.

9. *The transition from the kindergarten to the first grade
department should not be made too abruptly.* Some activities should be planned which are very similar to those
enjoyed in the previous department. For example, if during
the course of a Sunday morning, the kindergarteners are
used to having light refreshments (perhaps milk and cookies),
then occasionally this should be done in the early weeks in

the first-grade department.   Some of the same songs should
be sung in the new department.   If the previous department
had any pet characters, such as puppets, perhaps one of
those characters could visit the Sunday school department
and this will enable the children to feel less strange.

All of the children have to learn to grow up.   The leaders
of the new department should certainly plan each Sunday's
activities so that the changes will not be such that will drive
the children away, but will rather interest them in continuing
to attend the new department.

Division of Classes

1. *Boys meet together in classes and are taught by Christian gentlemen.* It is very wise to begin early in the grading
of the Sunday school with men teachers for boys.   In the
First Baptist Church of Hammond a boy has a man teacher when he enters first grade, and from then on he is taught
by men.   No lady teaches a man or a boy the Word of
God after he becomes a first grader.   It is not our intention
to raise sissies for God.   It is our desire to raise men for
God.   The men who teach these boys should dress, act,
live, and teach in a way that the boys can hope and plan
to become just like their teacher.

2. *Girls meet together in classes and are taught by fine
Christian ladies.*   It is important at this age level to give
the girls an opportunity to have a lady who teaches just
girls and who cares about their problems. The lady teachers should dress, live, teach, and conduct themselves in a
way that they can be examples for the girls to follow.

3. *The classes are divided by areas for the sake of convenience in visitation.*   Because we are located in the downtown area of Hammond, Indiana, most of our people live
some distance from our church property.   Consequently, it
would be possible for a teacher to have boys in his class
that live many, many miles from each other.   For this
reason we find it wise to divide our classes by areas so
that within a given number of hours a teacher is able to
accomplish more visiting.   Also, the boys who bring friends
from their neighborhood will have the privilege of having
their visitors in the same class with them.   Children who

come on their own are more likely to find someone in the class they already know from school, the neighborhood playground, etc., if the classes are divided by areas.

4. *The superintendent should carefully and prayerfully select the teacher for each class after dividing them by gender and by areas.* She should consider what the needs of the boys and girls in that area may be and what teacher could best meet these needs.

It is often helpful if a teacher can teach a class whose area includes her own home. This will enable her to do much more calling and also will make it easier to plan social activities for the children in her class. The children are also more likely to see their teacher in everyday life — on the street, at the neighborhood stores, etc. The teacher can have a good influence on his class throughout the week.

Departmental Setup

1. *Our staff consists of a superintendent, two secretaries, two general teachers (one lady and one man), and thirteen regular teachers.* This is our staff at the time of this writing.

2. *We are located on the top floor of Miller Hall.* Our room arrangement is shown below.

(Illustration on next page)

A. **Assembly room**
B. **Classrooms**
C. **Rest rooms**
D. **Storage**
E. **Speaker stand**
F. **Piano**

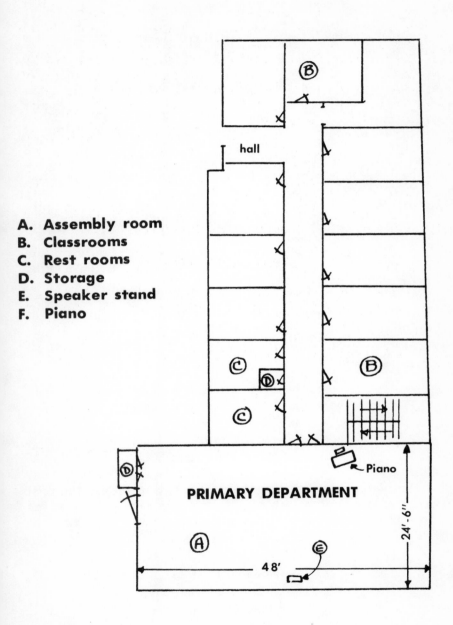

The seven teachers who have classrooms are rotated annually with the six teachers who meet in the assembly room divisions. Divisions for these classes are made after the opening assembly period by pulling accordion doors.

The Opening Assembly

1. *Begin on time.* If Sunday school is announced to begin at 9:40, the opening assembly should not begin at 9:41. It should begin at 9:40. Lateness in beginning the hour not only wastes the time of the people who come on time, but it encourages people to come late all the time.

2. *The opening assembly should last no more than twenty minutes.* This includes the dismissal of classes. Promptly at ten o'clock our classes should be in session for the remainder of the Sunday school hour.

3. *Have a well-planned opening assembly.* My outline has usually been as follows: Sing a little. Teach a little. Promote a lot!

4. *Sing a little.* Boys and girls love to sing, especially if most of the songs are familiar to them. We sing several familiar choruses, and we also sing a welcome song to our visitors. Each visitor stands and the boys and girls join in singing for them:

There's a welcome here, a welcome here,
There's a Christian welcome here.
Hallelujah!
There's a welcome here, a welcome here,
There's a Christian welcome here!

We also recognize those who have had birthdays the past week. We sing our birthday song to them. We use the traditional tune and sing the following words:

Happy birthday to you
Only one will not do;
Take Christ as your Saviour
And then you'll have two.

Each child who stands in honor of his birthday is privileged to tell how old he became that week. Personal attention is given to these boys and girls, and the song is sung for them.

The singing of songs in the Primary I Department should be both delightful and spiritual. For example, instead of simply announcing, "Now we will sing 'Jesus Loves Me,'" it would be well for the superintendent to ask first of all, "How many of you boys and girls love Jesus?" After they have raised their hands, she could say, "You love Him because He loves you. I know a song that tells us that Jesus loves us. Do you know one? Let's sing it. Let's sing, 'Jesus Loves Me, This I Know.'"

In turn, the superintendent could encourage the children to let Jesus know they love Him. The words of the chorus could be changed very slightly and the children could join their hearts and voices in singing:

> Yes, I love Jesus,
> Yes, I love Jesus,
> Yes, I love Jesus,
> I love to tell Him so.

Every effort should be made to make the singing in Primary I meaningful but also full of praise and delight.

5. *Teach a little.* The superintendent should have clearly in mind what new concept, song, Bible verse, lesson, etc., she intends to teach the boys and girls during each Sunday morning's opening assembly. She should not try to teach them so many things that they cannot remember any of them. One main point should be well taught and well learned. For this reason I use the phrase "teach *little.*"

It may be that the superintendent may want to teach a new song. If this is what she has planned for the particular Sunday morning, then she should teach it well and teach it thoroughly. She should teach it early in the twenty-minute period. Then after recognizing the visitors and honoring those who have had birthdays, she could have the children sing the new song again. She could continue her opening assembly by having her usual time of promotion, and just before the children go to their classes, she could have them sing the new song again. In other words, if it is her purpose to teach a new song, she should capitalize upon this purpose and do it thoroughly and right.

If the superintendent has prepared an object lesson for presentation in the opening assembly, she should be careful not to make too many applications. Boys and girls will not remember any of them if too many are taught. It would be best to present a brief, interesting object lesson which makes clear a scriptural truth and let it go at that. It is far better to teach one truth well than to make so many applications and have those poorly taught.

Boys and girls love to hear stories, and from time to time the superintendent may choose to tell a short story during the opening assembly time. If she does, she must be careful to watch the clock. Stories are fun and exciting to tell, and a good storyteller may get so involved with her story that she fails to realize that time is slipping by. Regardless of how effective a superintendent is with boys and girls, she should not be delinquent about obeying the rule of holding the opening assembly time to twenty minutes at a maximum.

Re-emphasizing our rule "teach a little," may I suggest that only one of the following teaching techniques be used per Sunday: the giving of an object lesson, the teaching of a new song, the telling of a short story, the teaching of an extra Bible memory verse, etc.

6. *Promote a lot.*   Here is perhaps the greatest responsibility of the departmental superintendent. It is her job to create a departmental team spirit within her department. She must develop enthusiasm for growth. Departmental *esprit de corps* is vital for growth in any age department, but especially for boys and girls of young age.

Departmental spirit is very important when the boys and girls are first new in a particular department. They are used to calling the name of their previous department, and they must become very familiar with the name of the new department.   In order to accomplish this, in the opening assembly of the first three or four Sundays with my new boys and girls, I spend a few moments each time helping the boys and girls learn to say "Primary I."   First of all

I tell them the name of our new department. Then I ask them to repeat it to me. I then ask them to tell each other. Then I ask them to tell the teacher. Then I ask them to hold up one finger and point that finger at me as they say each syllable of Pri-ma-ry I. I suggest to them that they invite their friends who are going to be in first grade as well as their neighbor friends who will be in kindergarten or second grade. Then very abruptly in the midst of my conversation I say, "To what department will you invite them?"

They all respond enthusiastically, "Pri-ma-ry I," shaking their fingers at me just as I had taught them to do. Anything that can indelibly and effectively place the name of the new department in their minds is important to do.

During the opening assembly, big days, departmental drives, contests, etc., should be announced enthusiastically. The superintendent could use posters, puppets, surprise guests, secret codes, etc., to announce big days. She should never simply say, "Next Sunday will be very important. We want everyone here."

Rather, she should say, "Do you know what day next Sunday is? It is June 23. Say that with me, boys and girls. Ready?"

"June 23."

"Can the teachers say it?"

"June 23."

"What day is next Sunday, boys and girls?"

"June 23."

The boys and girls will get the idea that on the twenty-third of June something wonderful is going to happen. The superintendent can then further explain what will happen on June 23 by telling it with much expression or by having some object or picture there to describe what will happen. Using the appropriate articles, she could say something like this: "O-o-o-oh, this sunbonnet will help keep the sun out of my eyes. The sun is so hot this summer, but it will not make me miss Sunday school! I do not want you to miss Sunday school either. Next Sunday, June 23, might be a hot day. Just because it might be hot, we are going to do something special for you. See this package of Kool-aid? See this ice-cube tray? See this package of cookies? Every teacher is going to bring cookies and Kool-aid next Sunday. What day?"

"June 23."

"Oh, I see. February 10."

"No, June 23."

"Oh, I see. We are going to have cookies and Kool-aid on July 19."

"No. No."

"Well, what day is it?"

"JUNE 23!"

"Oh, I see. December 15."

"No-o-o-o-o-o-o."

"Well, boys and girls, you must tell me once more. Mrs. Colsten just doesn't seem to learn. What day?"

"June 23."

"Oh, yes, and we are having snowballs."

"No, no."

"What are we having?"

"Kool-aid and cookies."

"Wonderful. What day?"

"June 23."

You can readily see that the boys and girls will not forget that on the 23rd of June they will have cookies and Kool-aid. All of that may seem a bit juvenile to the adult reader of this book, but aren't we teaching juveniles? Aren't we teaching little boys and girls? Why shouldn't we teach and lead in such a way that we will get children as excited about Sunday school and church as they are about the average television program?

In planning the presentation of promotional activities by means of posters and charts, the superintendent should be conscious of the reading level of her Primary I boys and girls. As the school year progresses, she can use more words, of course, because they will have learned to read better. In the days preceding their days in public school first grade and in the early days of their first-grade experiences, she should utilize many pictures and repeat simple words on her charts. It would be very wise for the superintendent of Primary I boys and girls to secure a vocabulary list from the basic readers used in the local school so that she may utilize a great many of the same words that the boys and girls are learning in public school. She should also make use of these words in departmental mailings that she sends to the boys and girls as well as on the charts, posters, etc., that she uses in the departmental assembly.

7. *Dismissal to classes.* At the close of the opening assembly time I call upon one of the gentlemen to lead in prayer. Of course, all of the boys and girls are very quiet and very settled. With this attentiveness still intact the superintendent may dismiss the classes by colors (according to their name tags). Each class files out of the assembly room in orderly fashion. Those classes which remain in the divided assembly room for their class sessions are instructed to wait to close the accordion doors until I give the signal.

Boys and girls love discipline and need it. Children who do not get discipline and act in a rowdy manner may appear to be enjoying the chaos, but they really do not. Boys and girls want and need strong leadership.

Departmental Records

1. *Each teacher has a small packet in which he keeps his attendance cards.* A blue card is made for each child on his roll. This card is made in our church office. An example is shown below.

Name												
Address												
Teacher				Grade				Year				

June				July				August			
September				October				November			
December				January				February			
March				April				May			

You can see that an entire year's attendance record can be kept on this card.

2. *Each visitor who comes to our department is registered.* The secretaries take down his name, address, and any other information that he may know about himself such as phone number, birthdate, etc. They make a carbon copy of this and retain the carbon copy for my use as superintendent. They send the original copy with the child as they introduce him to his teacher and show him where he may sit. As the teacher becomes acquainted with the child, he puts this visitor's registration slip in his packet. When this packet is returned to the secretaries after attendance is taken, the secretaries make a blue attendance card so that every time thereafter that child attends Primary I he does not feel like a visitor, but rather he feels that he belongs.

3. *As soon as each teacher has taken attendance he fills out the attendance slip shown below.*

Date_____

Class_____
Members Present_____
Visitors Present_____
Teacher Present_____

Total Present_____

Bibles Brought_____
Visits Made_____
Phone Calls Made_____
Cards Sent_____

One child is chosen from the class to bring the slip and the packet to the departmental desk. There one of the secretaries tallies the information on a sheet which is made in triplicate. One sheet is retained in the departmental records; one sheet is turned into the church office for the church records; and one sheet is given to me personally as superintendent.

4. *It is the responsibility of the superintendent to keep an up-to-date mailing list of the boys and girls in her department.* Initially she has a mailing list from the list of names and addresses given to her by the previous department on Promotion Day. From time to time she can use the words "Return Requested" on her mailings to the boys and girls. This way she can receive from the post office any available forwarding addresses. Her teachers should also be very prompt in reporting to her any changes of address or any situations where the family has moved far away. The teachers, of course, find these bits of information as they do their visiting, and they should inform their superintendent of the same. The superintendent must also be prompt in adding visitors' names and addresses to her current mailing list each week so that the new boys and girls get in the mailings from the department.

5. *Each teacher should have a complete up-to-date list of his own class available at home.* He should not have to have his packet at home in order to be aware of the boys in his class. Often the packet is needed by the superintendent and secretaries to keep information up-to-date. For this reason the teacher should have at home a complete list of the children in his class. He can use this for visitation purposes as well as in his daily prayer time.

Teacher-Pupil Relationship

1. *Though the teacher will endeavor to be a pal to his boys, he must remember that firm discipline is essential.* An orderly-conducted class is vital. Even roll call should be conducted in a businesslike manner. The rules the teacher would like followed in the class procedure should be made simple and clear. You see, first graders are easily taught, but they need the security of consistent leadership.

2. *It should be obvious to the boys and girls in each teacher's class that they are loved deeply, prayed for sincerely, and cared about by their teachers.*

3. *The teacher should visit in the home of every pupil on his roll as soon as possible.* Immediately upon receiving a class list the teacher should begin visiting the children in his class. He should not wait for a child to be an absentee. He should be careful to make calls on children of faithful church members as well. Many times the children of faithful families are overlooked because a visit is not considered essential to the child's attendance. However, every Sunday school teacher makes an impression on the child, and this impression should be a good, lasting one.

4. *The teacher should be an example to whom the child can look for guidance, love, and Christian leadership.* The manner of attire and conduct on the part of the teacher should not only be above reproach, but should be the very best.

5. *Learn and keep a written record of each child's birthday, phone number, vacation plans, pets, favorite foods and colors, and family members.* Yes, a teacher should get to know his children well!

6. *The teacher should pray regularly for each child by name.* Each child should be prayed for at least once a week. In some cases, the class is small enough for each teacher to pray for each child every day if he will discipline himself to do so. In an extremely large class the teacher could follow a cycle and pray perhaps for five or ten names each day of the week.

7. *The teacher should have planned social activities regularly.* He may do this in any number of ways. He may do some of this on an individual basis. Depending on the size of the class he may choose to have a personal social activity for each child in his class one time during the year. For example, he may take one boy out for pitch and catch each Saturday until he has had an "appointment" with each boy. In the case of a lady teacher, she may choose to have a different girl from her class home with her for Sunday dinner each week. Of course, many ideas along this line could be suggested, but the important thing is that the teacher should spend time with the pupils individually

as well as in a group.

If the teacher's class area is rather large, perhaps covering several suburbs, he may have a social time with the boys in one area one Saturday and those from another area the next, etc. The complete class, however, should have something planned all together with the teacher at least once each quarter. A class should have more to remember than a mere Christmas party after they have left our departments. There should be much feeling of unity.

8. *The teacher should take his class members on visitation with him.* For example, Mr. Gifford could call and make arrangements to meet Bobby at his home at three o'clock on Saturday afternoon. He could stop by for Bobby and take him along to visit three or four of the class members in the same general area. After making the visits he may stop by a refreshment stand and purchase an ice cream cone or some sort of refreshment for Bobby and himself. This would give the teacher and the boy a feeling of comradeship. The boy has not only been able to visit prospective class members with his teacher, but he has learned to go soul winning. This is vital. In the little social time following the visitation, the boy has had an opportunity to spend a few minutes chatting with his teacher, and, of course, the teacher has become better acquainted with the boy and his needs. Of course, the teacher should always have the boy back home at the time agreed upon with his parents. This could be a highly valuable time for the boys and girls and one to which they would look forward with anticipation. After all, an appointment with a Sunday school teacher is something very big!

9. *The teacher should be alert to the spiritual needs of his children.* He should observe his children with special care. He should observe the children's progress spiritually. He should be aware of the decisions they make in the public church services. For example, when a man sees a boy in his class is under conviction and ready to accept Christ as Saviour, he should be prompt to lead him to the Lord. If the family is unchurched, he should make a visit promptly and encourage baptism. When the child is baptized, he should make mention of this in the class. He should tell the other boys, "Jack was baptized. Isn't that fine? He

obeyed the Lord. After we are saved we should be baptized immediately."

The teacher should watch closely to see other times when a child has indicated spiritual progress. Perhaps in a Sunday evening service at invitation time the child has gone to the altar to pray privately. If the teacher is alert to this sort of thing, he can speak to the child after the service and simply encourage him to stay close to the Lord and always be willing to pray at the altar. Perhaps the teacher and the boy could be seated in one of the church pews and have a brief word of prayer for the child to continue to grow in grace.

10. *The teacher should send personal Christmas cards and other special occasion cards.* Each teacher should plan to send each child in his class a card on his birthday. If any child has won any particular honor, the teacher should be alert to send him a word of congratulations.

11. *When the teacher takes a summer vacation, he should send each child in his class a note or a picture postcard while he is gone.* This will help to keep the class attendance up and will also assure the children that the teacher is thinking of them.

12. *In case of a child's illness, the teacher should visit, write, or phone the child regularly.* Many a child has been lost to the Sunday school because during a prolonged illness there was no contact with the Sunday school and when he got well he did not care about coming back. No one encouraged him and no one showed any interest. This is very sad!

13. *At the close of the year the teacher should write each child a personal note.* The teacher should express what a wonderful privilege it was to have him in his class, encourage him to grow spiritually, remind him to be faithful to the next class and teacher, and reassure him of the teacher's continued love, prayers, and interest as the child grows older.

This may seem needless to say, but nevertheless it is true: Every person who is now doing a work for God was at one time six years old. Someone influenced his life at that early age. It is a very impressionable age. It is a vital age! The very best of teaching should occur in the early years of childhood. No teacher should regard carelessly the privilege and responsibility of teaching first-grade boys and girls.

Of course, every age is important, and each teacher makes his impression for bad or good, mediocrity or excellence, faithfulness or carelessness in the life of each child. May every Primary I teacher and superintendent around the world determine to do his best to accomplish the most for Christ in the life of each precious little first grader.

15. The Junior Department

(Written by Mrs. Lewis Shoaf, Superintendent of the Junior I
Department, First Baptist Church, Hammond, Indiana)

Duties of a Junior Departmental Superintendent

Every superintendent should be 100% behind the pastor
and the work of the church. Big decisions should never be
made without first discussing the matter with the pastor. A
superintendent should also keep the members of her own
family interested in her department.

1. *Make teaching a pleasure, not a chore.* The superintendent should make teaching as pleasant as possible for
her teachers.   Checking the classroom for erasers, chalk,
chairs, flannelgraph boards, etc., will help the teachers.
Registering new pupils before going to the classroom is an
asset to the teacher.   Encourage each teacher to decorate
his classroom.   Should any teacher fail to do so, the superintendent should take this responsibility to make the room
attractive for the pupils.   Praise a job well done.   Never
show discouragement. The superintendent should not expect
too much from her teachers — financially or physically.
Use husband and wife teachers as much as possible and
assign them the same teaching area.

2. *Keep teachers informed.* It is the responsibility of
the superintendent to make certain that all teachers and
workers are informed of any changes made in the department.   When planning a departmental teachers' meeting
(usually only two or three are necessary for the year), or
any other activity, everyone should know the date, time,

and place of meeting at least a week in advance. A teachers' meeting could be planned for Sunday afternoon about two hours before the evening service. This will save the teachers and workers an extra night away from their families. Have the entire staff attend this meeting. The teachers and workers should each have a copy of the name, address, and phone number of the entire staff in the department.

3. *What shall be expected from the teachers.* Teachers are expected to be faithful to all the services. They should love their pupils, be burdened for them, and seek to win them to the Lord. They are required to visit in the homes of each absentee and visitor weekly. Teachers should keep their records up to date and inform the superintendent if a pupil has moved or is attending another Bible-believing church. No teacher is to have an inactive list. All inactive pupils are to be treated as active pupils. The name of an inactive pupil is not to be removed from the class records until all possible means have been used to get the pupil back in Sunday school. Teachers are to notify the superintendent as far in advance as possible when planning to be out of town.

4. *Be conscious of lost souls in the department.* Oftentimes the pupil with the biggest discipline problem is not only seeking attention but is really wanting someone to show him the way of salvation. The superintendent should make the way of salvation clear during the opening assembly either by explaining it through a song, object lesson, story, etc. She should invite the pupils to tell their teachers if they are not sure they have been born again. It is nothing unusual for a teacher to tell me he has led a pupil to the Lord in his Sunday school class. This happens almost every Sunday in our department.

5. *Be enthusiastic.* Enthusiasm and smiles are contagious. Juniors love enthusiasm. Always look for juniors wherever you go and greet them warmly. They are pleased when they see you on the street or in a store.

6. *Be an example to the teachers.* Every superintendent should have taught several years in the Sunday school to know exactly what her teacher faces. She should be consecrated and dedicated to her work as well as an example to her entire staff. The superintendent should be willing to

do more than her share of the work if necessary. She should not expect from others what she would not do herself. She should set the pace for her department. Her example in conduct, dress, work, and faithfulness will influence her department. She must be willing to sacrifice and share her time whenever needed. The superintendent should be the first one to arrive in the department on Sunday mornings and make sure everything is in readiness for the day.

8. *Work the department all year long.* Never expect a summer slack, a holiday slump, or bad weather low attendance. Work harder during these times than ever before. During the spring and fall contests teachers and pupils will help carry the load, but the superintendent must bear the weight the rest of the time. During every opening assembly she should always have something exciting to say about the next Sunday and some future event coming up in a few weeks.

9. *Set high goals.* Plan to nearly double your attendance from what you had on Promotion Day. Plant this goal and desire in the hearts of your teachers and pupils. Talk about it each week. During contest weeks, set goals for each class and for the entire department. Honor the classes who reach their goals.

10. *Share responsibilities as they increase.* The superintendent should not allow herself to become so burdened with detail duties that the more important things are neglected. The superintendent should free herself from registering visitors, teaching, figuring percentages, and other duties which are time-consuming. Secretaries, substitute teachers, and helpers should share in these responsibilities.

11. *Departmental letters should be sent often.* Every junior boy and girl likes to receive mail. When promoting something special in the department, the superintendent should send a departmental letter to each pupil enrolled in the department. This includes all who attend faithfully, all who do not, each visitor, and each departmental staff member. The letter should include an attractive picture, a short description of the special event, the name of the church, department, location, and date. If using a postage permit, the superintendent can take advantage of this and mimeo-

graph the permit and church return address on the back-side, fold, and address, thus avoiding the use of envelopes.

12. *Be thoroughly prepared at all times.* Start and dismiss opening assembly exactly on time. Never cheat a teacher of precious teaching time. Have each minute planned! If one minute is lost, the entire group is lost, thus creating discipline problems. During contest weeks, plan the entire contest before it begins. Be organized! Expect calamities and be prepared for them. Plan for future events.

Much time should be spent in preparation for the coming Sunday. The superintendent should have the songbooks with a slip of paper stating the songs and page numbers ready for the pianist. The pianist should begin playing five minutes before the opening assembly. Only the superintendent knows how much she has to accomplish in her opening assembly. She may have a teacher who would make a better songleader than she but who would take more time singing than can be spared. It is better that the superintendent lead her own singing and get her program across even though it may not be as good. The superintendent should keep a written copy of each of the opening assemblies and file according to date with the attendance written in the corner. An example of a twenty-minute opening assembly follows:

Date ————————

Attendance ————————

(1) Signal for reveille to be played on trumpet by teacher.

(2) "Attention" — pupils stand at attention.

(3) Songs: "I'm in the Lord's Army (*Salvation Songs for Children #3,* page 21) "On God's Word I'll Stand" (*Salvation Songs for Children #4,* page 35)

(4) I wonder how many of you boys and girls have had a birthday this past week. If you have, then come up and let us sing "Happy Birthday" (*Action,* page 51) to you. Birthday pencils are given to pupil before opening assembly to pass out to those having birthdays. Birthday cake to be put on

flannelgraph board by pupil is also given to pupil before opening assembly. When we sing about two birthdays, we are singing about the first time we were born. We were born into the family of our mothers and daddies and sisters and brothers. The second time is when we accept the Lord Jesus as our Saviour and are born into His family. Everyone must have two birthdays to go to Heaven. How many birthdays have you had?

(5) Boys and girls, look at our prayer puppet. He is going to shut his eyes while we pray. Every boy and girl in the room must shut his eyes and not talk while Mr. ————— (man teacher of the department) comes to lead us in prayer. (Prayer puppet is given to a pupil before opening assembly to hold during this prayer time.)

(6) CONTEST REPORT:
Look at Mount Victory! The girls are ahead by 1%! Boys, are you going to let the girls beat you? Girls, you are really going to have to work or the boys will pass you up next Sunday.

(7) SWORDS: (Good swords will be awarded to the boys' and girls' classes having the highest percentage gain. Broken swords are "awarded" to the classes having the least percentage gain.)
Today the classes taught by Mrs. ————— and Mr. ————— are awarded the good swords. Let's give them a hand.
My, how I hate to give out these broken swords. They go to the classes taught by Mrs. ————— and Mr. —————. Let's all say "ahhh." I'm sure you don't want a broken sword in your class next Sunday, do you? The only safe way to keep from getting one in your class is to come and bring others with you to Sunday school.

(8) SURPRISE BOX: "What do you think is in here?" You will never guess because it is a SURPRISE BOX. One will be given to the boy and one to the girl who bring the most absentees or visitors to his or her class next Sunday.

(9) COMING IN JUST 3 MORE SUNDAYS—"ICE

CREAM SUNDAE, SUNDAY" How many of you like ice cream sundaes? Good! Do you know that we are going to have an "Ice Cream Sundae, Sunday" here in our Junior I Department? The sundaes will be served between the Sunday school hour and the church service. I will be telling you more about it and will send you a letter telling you all about it in a couple of weeks.

(10) STORY: "The Tragedy That Inspired Victory"

(11) No junior boy or girl will leave the department after Sunday school unless accompanied by the teacher. Teachers may leave for classes. AT-TENTION! Junior I soldiers will march to classes beginning with the front row.

13. *Check individual class attendances weekly.* Have the secretaries make a carbon copy of the attendance sheet for the superintendent. Check class attendances and teachers' packets regularly. Pupils should not be allowed to slip into the wrong class unless exception has been made by the superintendent or the head secretary. This would often mean that the pupils from another area will not get visited. Teachers must leave their packets at the church on Sundays and can pick them up Wednesday at the regular Teachers' and Officers' Meeting if they so desire.

14. *Pinpoint weak spots in the department.* If the superintendent checks her class attendances and packets weekly, she can almost always tell which teacher is working and which is not. She can tell which teachers could take bigger areas. When a teacher often sends pupils to her for discipline, the superintendent has a right to feel this teacher is either not as prepared as he should be, cannot control his pupils, or is unable to handle a very big class. The superintendent must keep these things in mind at promotion time and place each teacher according to his ability. Watch each teacher's interest in his pupils. Does the teacher sit and talk with his pupils before the opening assembly? Is the teacher eager to see his pupils or does he visit with another teacher? Is he faithful to the Teachers' and Officers' Meeting on Wednesday nights? When he has missed a Sunday, does he call and ask how many were in his class and check who was absent? When a class seems to

be at a standstill, it is the superintendent's place to call in the homes and find out why the pupils are not coming. If she finds half of the pupils enrolled are not attending and have no interest, it is advisable to divide the class. She should talk to the teacher about his class and remind him of his promise to visit when he became a teacher. She may suggest that he divide his class, giving the new teacher as many active pupils as he keeps. The superintendent should never try to divide a class on her own, for she does not know the pupils and their relationship with their teacher. Dividing a class in the middle of the year can be a very serious thing and may cause some pupils not to return.

15. *Give new teachers and workers in the department an opportunity to become orientated.* When a new teacher or substitute teacher comes to your department, have him sit in a classroom with one of your teachers the first Sunday or two. Inform the veteran teacher of his coming in advance. The teacher can show and tell the new teacher little detail things which are done in the department which the superintendent may forget to mention.

16. *Have each classroom numbered and have the teacher's name printed on the door.* This can add to the attractiveness of your department as well as make your teacher feel it is his own personal room. Our teachers pay the expense of having their name plates printed. Name plates should read, MR. TERRY WRIGHT or MRS. HARRY DAVIS. Never use the teacher's first name. Having the rooms "named and numbered" is helpful to both pupils and workers in the department.

17. *General teachers are to be as diligent as regular teachers.* The same rules apply for general teachers as regular teachers. They are expected to be prepared to teach at all times. Secretaries are also expected to be prepared to teach should an emergency arrive. Classes should *never* be combined. This is admitting defeat and is certainly unfair to the class. The general teacher should be called at the earliest date possible. He should be informed of the classroom number, teacher's name, and area he will be teaching. A typewritten list of general teachers and their designated classes should be posted on the bulletin board

along with a list of teachers who are available to teach.

18. *Have jobs for everyone.* Keep your staff busy. Never let anyone be idle. If this should ever happen, let him help clean the assembly room while pupils are in their classes. Make everyone feel he is needed and that his job is important, for it is!

19. *Be on constant lookout for improvements.* The superintendent should read everything she can find. She should seek ideas from other superintendents, pastors, and teachers. The teachers should know she is anxious to get their ideas. It should be made easy for the teachers to give their suggestions to her either personally or by the use of a suggestion box or a designated place in the department.

20. *The superintendent and her staff should have a good relationship.* The superintendent should pray daily for her entire departmental staff. She should love each one and be burdened for each one. When one of the staff is in the hospital, flowers should be sent by the superintendent from the department. An offering can be taken in a teachers' meeting to cover this expense. Birthday cards should be sent by the superintendent from the teachers and officers of the department with an added note of appreciation. Congratulatory cards are sent to those having babies.

The superintendent should never show partiality to her teachers. She should avoid jealousy among her teachers. It is her place to build up a good interstaff relationship with each other. She should make them feel they are the best group of teachers anywhere and that she couldn't do without them. Each one is needed in his own particular area.

It is not wise to have lady teachers compete against each other, or men teachers compete against men teachers. It is best to have all lady teachers working together in competition against all the men teachers. The superintendent should make rules for the department and expect them to be carried out.

21. *"Lost and Found" articles should be handled efficiently.* Juniors are careless, and many things are left in the department. Assign someone in charge of the lost and found. Our custodian cares for this for us and keeps a list on all articles left in the department.

Departmental Promotion and Setup of Classes

Departmental promotion can be one of the most crucial times for the department. The superintendent must keep in mind that all teachers do not have the same abilities and must be placed accordingly.

1. *Divide classes according to areas.* Give each teacher an opportunity to state the desired area he would like to work for the coming year with the understanding that bus captains, bus drivers, and visitation captains have first choice of areas. Place the teacher as near the desired area as possible. It is a waste of your teachers' time to live in one area and be expected to make weekly visits in another area far from home.

Get a large city map from the City Hall and a listing of the school districts from the School Board. Outline each school district in a different colored pencil and shade the block in which the school is located on the map. Post this in a convenient place so the teachers may refer to it when looking for street locations.

Assign pupils according to school areas in city limits and according to suburban areas outside of city limits. It may be necessary to divide some school areas into two classes or combine two or three schools. This will depend on the number of pupils coming from that particular area. This will make it possible for your pupils to know someone in their Sunday school class and take away the fear of being alone. It will strengthen the pupils to live for the Lord at school, and it also makes them conscious of schoolmates who do not attend Sunday school. Placing a new pupil in the wrong class may mean losing him forever.

2. *Start your classes small.* Do not burden your teachers on Promotion Day with a big enrollment. It is far better to curtain your assembly room, divide present rooms, use buses for classrooms or utilize other means of division than to expect the impossible from your teachers. Begin each class with an average active enrollment of six or seven, but assign all inactive names and addresses from the specific area to the teacher of that class. Expect the classes to double in attendance, especially those in the city.

3. *Never have an inactive list as such.* As a rule, inactive

pupils are a result of a neglectful teacher. Never allow an inactive list. Teachers are expected to treat the inactive pupils as they do the active in visitation, parties, etc. The inactive pupil may come one Sunday for a special day and accept the Lord as his Saviour, thus changing and saving his entire life.

4. *Prepare teachers and pupils for Promotion Day.* Each teacher should be given a typewritten list of his new pupils (names, addresses, and phone numbers) the Sunday before promotion takes place. A letter should be sent to each incoming pupil telling where the new department is located and how the teacher and superintendent are looking forward to seeing them the coming Sunday. Plan something special for the first day in the new department. Sing songs that are familiar to the new pupils. Teachers' packets and new attendance cards should be typed for each class by the Wednesday night before promotion takes place.

5. *Have teachers, helpers, and secretaries greet new pupils promoted from another department.* By having each child greeted warmly and shown where to sit in the assembly the new pupils will feel more at ease.

6. *Make the first Sunday an impressive Sunday.* Avoid as much confusion as possible. Call your new classes by school areas and outlying areas. Have the teacher stand as his name is called. Announce the classroom number and the location of his classroom. Have all pupils living in that area to follow their new teacher to their class.

7. *Have a contest with your teachers immediately after promotion.* Have the lady teachers compete with the men teachers in a contest to see who can call in the homes of all their pupils first. Set a deadline. The losers treat the winners to a wiener roast. Husbands and wives are invited but are charged a small fee if they do not belong to the department. Have plenty of lively games, plenty to eat, and a songfest by the fire. This will encourage your teachers to call on their pupils soon after promotion. The outing must be planned in detail to be successful.

Promotional and Contest Sundays

Promotional Sundays are necessary throughout the year.

We have broken our all-time attendance record on holidays by promoting special Sundays. A promotional Sunday will only be as successful as the superintendent makes it. It must be thoroughly planned and publicized well in advance. One time, when planning a promotional Sunday, one teacher asked, "Won't the pupils come to Sunday school just because we are going to have a luncheon?" Yes, many pupils will come only for the little luncheon; however, they will get *more* than the luncheon. They will get a good lesson taught by the teacher, a good message on salvation by one of our pastors, and many will accept the Lord as their Saviour. Each teacher will receive new names and addresses for his class which will be good prospects. It is not all in vain!

Listed below are some promotional ideas we have used in our Junior I department:

1. *ICE CREAM SUNDAE, SUNDAY.* We serve the sundaes immediately after the Sunday school hour, but before the church service. Dixie cup ice cream (purchased), chocolate syrup (furnished by men teachers), chopped nuts (furnished by lady teachers), and whipped cream (furnished by the secretaries and helpers) are used. We use five serving tables going at one time. Each class lines up with their teacher. As the pupil takes the ice cream, one helper pours the chocolate syrup, another adds the nuts, and another, the whipped cream. Each class returns to their room with their teacher. All empty containers are put in large paper bags brought by the teacher. Approximately 600 pupils can be served in a very short period of time.

2. *LUNCHEON.* Wieners with buns (furnished by men teachers), barbeque with buns (furnished by lady teachers), catsup, mustard, relish, and potato chips (furnished by secretaries and helpers) can be served in the same manner as the ice cream sundaes but allow for a little more time.

3. *WORLD'S LARGEST CANDY BAR.* The candy bar can be made of two large sheets of cardboard taken from an empty carton. Place nine jumbo chocolate candy bars between. Wrap the ends with aluminum foil and the outside center with plain white shelf paper. Print WORLD'S LARGEST CANDY BAR in large letters on the wrapper. Use as an award for the pupil bringing the most absentees

to his class on a designated Sunday. Show it two or three Sundays before the presentation date.

4. *MOTHER'S DAY FLOWER.* Get a flat of petunias, or some other flower in bloom. Put each plant in a colorful paper cup with soil, and award to each pupil who brings a visitor or absentee. Also give one to each visitor.

5. *A TICKET TO THE ZOO OR MUSEUM.* Plan an outing for the department, but make the pupils come to Sunday school the previous Sunday to be eligible to go. Mimeograph tickets to be given the Sunday before the outing and give one to each pupil present. The ticket must state the event, time, meeting place, and time the group will return. The ticket should have a place for the signature of the parent and should be returned by the pupil when leaving for the trip. Have each pupil bring a sack lunch, and the teachers can furnish Kool-aid.

Plan the outing in detail. Have one sponsor for six pupils or less. Make sure each pupil is wearing an identification tag before he gets off the bus. The tag should have the name, address, and phone number of the church, as well as the name, address, and phone number of the pupil. Each bus should have a captain who will write the names of the pupils, teachers, and driver of her bus. Each teacher should make a list of the names of pupils in his charge. Let men teachers care for the boys and lady teachers care for the girls. The entire group need not stay together but all groups must know the designated time to return to the buses. Read the list of names before beginning the return trip to make sure every pupil is on the bus. When the buses arrive at the church, each teacher should stay until everyone in his group has been cared for.

6. *HAPPY BIRTHDAY PARTY.* This can be used to celebrate the birthday of a character in a story the superintendent has been telling, etc. Teachers bring cupcakes with candles, and balloons are left at the door of each classroom. Cupcakes are to be eaten in the classroom after Sunday school has been dismissed.

7. *KING AND QUEEN SUNDAY.* Make, or have made, two robes — one for the king and another for the queen. Crown the boy and girl with crowns (made from colored poster board and glitter) and put the robes on the honored

pupils. Take their picture with a Polaroid camera using colored film. Pupils may take the picture home with them. This can be used for the boy and girl bringing the most absentees, visitors, etc.

8. *BRING A FRIEND SUNDAY.* Have teachers carry placards which they made advertising, "Bring a Friend Sunday," and display the placards around the department the previous Sunday. Then give suckers to every pupil who brought a friend and to every visitor.

9. *JAPANESE SUNDAY.* Make Japanese lanterns from construction paper and give each pupil one to take home. Decorate the assembly room in Japanese fashion. Have a missionary from Japan speak during the opening assembly.

10. *SILLY BILLY AND OLD TIMER.* These characters are used in our vacation Bible school and loved by our juniors. They are usually in the department from seven to eight minutes.

11. *MOVING PICTURE SUNDAY.* Boys and girls like to see themselves on the screen. Set aside a Sunday to take moving pictures of the department. Promote this two or three Sundays in advance. Make another "big Sunday" when the pictures will be shown. We showed ours between the Sunday school hour and the church service.

12. *SANTA'S SAD HELPER GETS A NAME.* During the month of December build up "Santa's Sad Helper," who wants a name, but everyone is too busy to stop and give him a name. Have make-believe telegrams, letters, phone calls, etc., to build this up. Let the pupils give him a name by making pencils and paper available for them to write on before opening assembly and put in a large decorated box. Have Santa's helper come to the department and draw a name. Award a box of chocolates to the child whose name is chosen.

13. *SKITS.* Favorite T.V. characters such as Bat Man, Gomer Pyle, Beverly Hillbillies, etc., can be imitated to create much enthusiasm, but the skit should never last over eight minutes.

14. *SPECIAL FLANNELGRAPH STORIES.* Oftentimes the superintendent would like to tell the Easter and Christmas stories using scene-o-felt on the flannelgraph board. This may take an extra five or ten minutes of the teachers' time.

She should talk it over in teachers' meeting and take a vote. If the majority votes against it, she should omit it and forget it. However, most of them vote for the presentation as it portrays the beautiful Bible truths in colorful scenes and is impressive on the hearts and minds of the pupils. The superintendent must be careful not to take anything away from the lesson which the teachers have prepared to teach. This should never be done without the consent of the teachers.

15. *DEPARTMENTAL CONTEST.* Each contest must be prepared entirely at least two weeks before it begins. The success of a contest will depend on the superintendent. It should be announced and publicized greatly in advance. The contest should have a theme, a theme song, a goal for the department as a whole (high, but not too high to reach), and a goal for each class (usually figured on percentage). Each teacher should give the superintendent a written copy of what he is going to do in his class during contest weeks. The superintendent should make sure a copy is given to her by each teacher.

In the junior department, it is always good to have the boys compete against the girls. Have a chart, picture, or something to show the gain and loss of each team weekly. Treat the winning team. Award the winning class with the highest percentage gain and the losing class with the lowest percentage with a good and bad token respectively which correlates with the theme. Cheer for the good classes and everyone say "ahh" for the losing classes. No booing.

Secretarial Duties

The departmental secretary shares a big responsibility in the success of your department. It is most important that he knows what is expected of him. He must be cooperative with the superintendent and be patient, polite, and understanding with the pupils and fellow workers. His work must be neat, accurate, and up-to-date. The secretary should arrive early and have everything ready by the time the pupils begin to arrive. Be organized.

1. *Do not work short-handed.* If the department occupies more than one floor, there should be an attendance secretary

and as many helpers as needed for each floor.

2. *Appoint a head secretary.* In a large department it is impossible for the superintendent to care for the many detail duties. A head secretary can be very helpful. This is preferably a man, especially since it requires a lot of running around. The head secretary is responsible to see that some-one is assigned to stamp the hands of our bus pupils. He checks all classrooms to make sure all teachers are present. In the case of an emergency absence by a teacher the head secretary fills the position immediately from the names listed on the bulletin board. The head secretary takes the attend-ance and offering to the church office. It is his responsibility to see that it gets to the office in time. He also posts a man teacher at each entrance to make sure no pupil leaves the building once he has entered. He aids the secretaries with their needs and supplies. When pupils other than Junior I age come to the department, he takes them to their right department. When planning an outing, he gets the buses and bus drivers lined up. He gets the tables and things needed for a departmental luncheon the Saturday before the luncheon is to be served. He also cares for the micro-phones and helps maintain order in the department.

3. *Register new pupils before the opening assembly begins.* Registration is done only on the main floor of our depart-ment. Each secretary has a mimeographed directory listing the names of school or area, classroom number, and name of teacher. The pupil is registered by name, address, phone number, name of school, grade in school, the class he will attend, and the date. He is placed in a class according to the school he attends. A carbon copy is made of this and given to the superintendent. The pupil takes the original copy and gives it to his teacher when entering class.

A sample portion of our departmental directory is shown below:

JUNIOR I DEPARTMENT, June 2, 1968

— HAMMOND AREA —

GIRLS			BOYS		
SCHOOL	ROOM NO.	TEACHER	SCHOOL	ROOM NO.	TEACHER
Caldwell	100	Mrs. Healy	Caldwell	27	Mr. Bennett
Columbia	104	Mrs. King	Columbia	20	Mr. Abner
Edison	202	Mrs. Coberg	Edison	16	Mr. Drexler

— OUTLYING AREAS —

GIRLS			BOYS		
SCHOOL	ROOM NO.	TEACHER	SCHOOL	ROOM NO.	TEACHER
Calumet City, Gr. 3	218	Mrs. Douglas	Calumet City, Gr. 3	25	Mr. Penley
Calumet City, Gr. 4	107	Mrs. Frizzell	Calumet City, Gr. 4	10	Mr. McCarroll
Cedar Lake	212	Mrs. Myers	Cedar Lake	6	Mr. Hiles

The directory should be in alphabetical order according to school and should be kept up-to-date.

After new pupils have been registered a hostess takes the pupils to the teacher and introduces them to the teacher or another pupil in the class. This gives the new pupils a feeling of security in a strange place.

4. *The secretaries collect class attendance slips and offering.* Each teacher checks attendance and takes the offering immediately 'upon entering the classroom. The attendance packet, attendance slip, and offering envelope are left on the floor in front of the classroom and are picked up by the secretaries. The secretaries give the attendance slips to the attendance secretary, empty the offering in a money bag, and put a new slip (new date and classroom number are written on it) and the empty offering envelope in each packet for the following Sunday.

5. *Secretaries assist teachers and superintendent.* The secretaries assist the teachers in every way they can. They also help in addressing departmental letters. Each secretary has specified amount consisting of certain areas. The secretary types the name and address neatly and combines mail for sisters and brothers.

When we plan a departmental luncheon or treat, the secretaries are in charge of the tables and are responsible for getting plenty of help. They know which table they will work and what is expected of them. Time is a very important factor and cannot afford to be wasted because of poorly organized help. On special occasions when treats and awards are to be given, the secretaries will leave these at the door of each classroom. At no time is the classroom door to be opened during the teaching unless it is to let in a pupil who arrives late.

6. *Keep a "Dead File."* This file is not for inactive pupils, for no such file should be kept. This file is only for pupils who have moved away, who are attending another Bible-believing church, or whose parents refuse to let them come again.

7. *Use pigeonhole mailboxes for teachers.* Pigeonhole mailboxes are convenient for the superintendent. This saves her having to see each teacher personally or calling each one on the phone. Packets, notes, announcements, returned letters, etc., can be placed in the boxes. Each pigeonhole is labeled with the teacher's name and classroom number.

Decorating the Department

Keeping the assembly room and halls of the department cheerful and attractive is wholly the responsibility of the superintendent. Use as much color as possible.

1. *Keep a file of pictures.* Children love pictures. Every superintendent should keep a file of pictures. This should include Bible pictures, seasonal pictures, and promotional material. The pictures should be large and colorful. Pictures should be hung at the eye level of the pupils and be changed several times a year. Never let a picture or sign hang crooked.

2. *Decorate the department for special days.* If you are having Japanese Sunday, make large Japanese letters from construction paper and put them on the wall, string paper lanterns across the room, and carry out your theme. If you are having a contest using armies as teams, use the Christian soldier and a silhouette of an American soldier. Use long sheets of crepe paper as background for your pictures. This will change the appearance of the room and give it freshness and color.

Decorate the walls with colorful leaves cut from construction paper and autumn pictures taken from magazines in the fall. In the winter months use winter snow scenes and snowflakes cut from white paper. In summer use flowers and summer scenes. The Christmas season is the choice time of the year because you can use much color. Make your department as decorative for Christmas as you can. Since we have space on both the main floor and the second floor in our department, we have a Christmas tree on both floors. Get a Christmas tree large enough for the department and decorate it beautifully. Artificial flowers also add much beauty to a department.

3. *Make attractive posters.* Get a small, inexpensive enlarger, and enlarge simple pictures on colored poster board. Paint them with water paints, and you will be surprised what this will do for your department.

4. *Use neat lettering on all signs.* Oftentimes you will have a teacher volunteer to do lettering for you. If you consent, then you must use it. However, it is best to buy large letter guides and do the lettering yourself. A neatly printed banner adds much to the theme and can be used effectively on a promotional day. Make the lettering large enough to be seen across the room.

Floor Plan of Junior Department

Our Junior I Department occupies an entire building which consists of a basement, main floor, and a second story. Our large assembly room is on the main floor. Classrooms are located on all floors.

16. Special Classes

There are many people in every city that could not be happily situated in any of the usual departments or classes provided by the Sunday school. The reaching of these people should certainly be given serious consideration by every pastor and Sunday school superintendent. There are many such classes provided by the First Baptist Church in Hammond, Indiana.

1. *The Deaf Department*

One of the most blessed works of our church is the work with the deaf. The director of this work is Miss Maxine Jeffries, a full-time paid member of our staff. Concerning the deaf work Miss Jeffries submits the following:

DEAF WORK

How to find a leader for the deaf:

To start a deaf work in your church find someone who has a burden and concern for the deaf. Since most people cannot communicate with the deaf, provisions will have to be made for their learning of the sign language. Find someone to come to your church and teach the sign language to prospective workers. If this is not possible, send your workers to the Bill Rice Ranch, Murfreesboro, Tennessee, to learn the sign language at their summer school.

How to generate enthusiasm in the church for a deaf work:

As with any ministry within the local church it is up to the pastor to bring the need before the people. Before the deaf class was started at the First Baptist Church, Hammond, Indiana, the pastor, Dr. Jack Hyles, sent out letters to all known deaf in our area telling them that on October 14, 1962, a very important new class was being established just for them. Saturday night, October 13, the deacons met and went two-by-two to each deaf home with a letter introducing themselves and inviting the deaf to come the next morning to their new class.

How to find the deaf:

There are many places to find the deaf. Listed here are a few suggestions:

(1) Ask the members of your church if they know of any deaf folks.

(2) Write the school for the deaf in your state and ask if they would give you the names of the deaf and hard-of-hearing in your area.

(3) Check in factories, printing shops, newspaper offices, shoe repair shops, I.B.M. installations, etc. The deaf students study primarily these vocations in their schools.

(4) Contact your Board of Education for names of deaf enrolled in "special" classes.

(5) Write to the Bill Rice Ranch, Murfreesboro, Tennessee, and ask them to send you a list of names of deaf people they know from your area and state. (They have a camp for the deaf and have a list of names from every state.)

If you find one deaf in your area, you have the key to finding other deaf because they are a society in themselves. Everywhere you go, ask people if they know any deaf folks. Get into the habit of asking, "Do you know any deaf folks?"

How to divide the classes:

As the new deaf work grows and workers are enlisted, more classes are formed. The Deaf Department of the First Baptist Church, Hammond, Indiana, now has seven classes for the deaf and hard-of-hearing. They are divided as follows:

    Children's Classes

        Primary ----------------------Ages 5, 6, 7
        Junior-----------------------Ages 8, 9, 10
        Intermediate Class --------Ages 11, 12, 13
        Teen-age Class--------------Ages 14 - 19

Adult Classes
   Adult Lip-reading Class
   Ladies' Bible Class
   Men's Bible Class

We are training deaf as well as hearing folk to teach in our Deaf Department. We have seven teachers — three of whom are deaf and four are hearing. All the officers — the president, vice-president, secretary, treasurer, and song-leader — of our Deaf Sunday School Department are deaf.

Our Sunday school classes are separate from the hearing but all preaching services are shared with the hearing. Every service is interpreted for the deaf and hard-of-hearing.

2. *The Spanish Class*
We have found that in our area many people cannot understand the English language because of their Mexican and Spanish background. Consequently, we provide classes taught in the Spanish language for these people. Concerning this work, the director, Mrs. Rose O'Brien has submitted the following:

THE SPANISH CLASS

The Spanish Class was formed in 1965. It came into being quite simply. One Sunday in the Pastor's Sunday school class, I offered my assistance to a lady by inter-preting for her from Spanish to English. Later that day the pastor asked me where I had learned to speak fluent Spanish. I replied, "I learned it in my home. Since my parents came from Spain and spoke only Spanish in our home, this was how I learned to speak it." The pastor then asked if I would like to teach a Sunday school class in Spanish. I replied in the affirmative, and my work began.

We found a desirable location and had only one prospect, but we started having our classes. With one in class and more prospects in mind we began a visitation program and began calling on Spanish-speaking people. This, of course, includes not only Spanish people, but Mexicans, Puerto Ricans, and Cubans. From this our class began to grow, and the Lord is blessing us constantly.

A few pointers or bits of advice which I would give are as follows:

(1) Accept the Spanish person as he is.

(2) Be punctual yourself thus teaching them by example.

(3) Study your Sunday school lesson well in order to translate it in such a manner that there is none of the meaning lost in the translation.

(4) Always use a Spanish person to teach the class as opposed to one who has learned the language in school. (I feel that a person who has been reared in· this particular environment understands better the feelings of these people and is more inclined to think like they do.)

(5) Be sure to organize groups from your class to do visitation and help them get started in this. As in anything else, once they see the results of their labors, their enthusiasm will grow.

(6) Form your own Women's Missionary Society Circle for the Spanish-speaking ladies.

(7) Do everything you can to make them feel a part of the entire church program, not just a separate section.

(8) Be patient with them as they are perhaps slower to learn and grasp things.

(9) Have your own officers just as any other class does.

(10) Always be the *leader* of your class, in all things doing exactly what the pastor says and the way he says it. Do it as gently as possible and as firmly as necessary.

3. *The Retarded Children*

One of the most blessed and inspiring works in all of our Sunday school is the work with the retarded children. This class is called the Sunbeam Class. Not only has it enabled us to reach many retarded children, but it has provided a way for their parents to come to Sunday school. The director of this work is Mrs. Zola Stevens. Mrs. Stevens writes concerning the work:

A CLASS FOR EDUCABLE, SLOW CHILDREN

The mentally retarded and their families represent a vast mission field, and it should be a challenge to any church as it has been to us here at First Baptist.

The mentally retarded are human beings, flesh and blood with real feelings and should be accepted for what they are and not for what they ought to be. Because of their short memory span and their short attention span, they cannot function with normal children effectively. You either meet the needs of the retarded child and neglect the others or visa-versa.

We started our class with four children already enrolled in our Beginner Department. I had to teach in that department only a few Sundays to see the need for a special class. At that time I didn't know it had ever been considered by the pastor, but later I was told that he had wanted a class started and had been praying for the Lord to send the right teacher. The Lord had already given me a burden for the mentally handicapped so I quickly volunteered.

The first thing we needed to look for was a suitable classroom — one located away from distractions as much as possible, well lighted, well ventilated, and with a rest room close by. After this was taken care of we felt we should visit in the homes of the children already enrolled and get the parents' permission to enroll them in a special class.

Workers were needed to help the teacher and the first requirement for selecting them is the spiritual one. Are they BORN-AGAIN Christians? Do they have a burden for the mentally handicapped? A teacher or a worker should have a special love for children, a stable personality, patience and courage. Personal mannerisms and voice are very important when dealing with retarded children. (The Lord can supply the needs if we are willing.) Two workers were found and approved by our pastor. One worker for every three or four children is the ratio that is recommended, and we find it to be necessary in order to have an organized class.

The teaching material for children with the chronological age of 5 through 12 had to be decided upon. Because the ability level for each child is not the same, we decided to use beginner and primary material and adapt it to the needs of the class. It is always necessary to repeat a lesson at least once and sometimes many times.

The schedule that we have followed from the beginning with slight variations from time to time is as follows:

9:40 — Greeting at the door, hang up coats, put on the name tags, and find a seat.

9:45 — Sing time. (They love to sing.)

9:55 — Prayer time, birthdays, and announcements.

10:00 — Lesson time.

10:30 — Memory work.

10:40 — Handwork (coloring) and take turns to the rest room.

11:00 — Sing time and special music.

11:10 — Refreshments.

11:30 — Handcraft.

11:50 — Story time.

12:10 — Play time.

12:30 — Coats on and special take-home gift selected and a candy treat handed out.

When a new child is enrolled it is important to find out the physical defects, seizures, medication, hearing ability, etc., of the child. We need to know what they are able to do for themselves and what transportation they used to get to church.

We have not found discipline to be a great problem. After a child has attended a few Sundays and knows what is expected of him, he usually tries to please. If a child is completely undisciplined in the home it takes much longer for them to adjust. From the beginning we established limits and rules. We try very hard to be consistent. When it is necessary to punish, we do it immediately and firmly with love. They need to know they are loved, in many cases they have known nothing but rejection. We reward good behavior. Many times a pat on the back or a smile can do wonders.

Because of our growth we have recently divided into two classes, separating the trainable and the educable children. God has been good because many of the educable children have been saved.

We have been given prospects by members of our church and their neighbors. The Lake County Association for Retarded Children has been helpful. Some private and public schools have allowed us to observe their teaching and hand out brochures for the students to take home.

Promotion for a special class is harder because of their

short memory span. We have found that a small take-home gift each Sunday is the best. We have used a Treasure Chest, Wishing Well, and a Surprise Box from which they may choose their take-home gifts.

One special big day was Mother's Day. In preparation for that day we took individual pictures of each child for two Sundays and then on the big day they made picture frames for handcraft and took the pictures home to Mom for Mother's Day.

In a recent Sunday school promotion where an Indian theme was used, we made a canoe, Indian, and a paddle for each child. They were thrilled to see their canoes move across the river each Sunday they attended. All that finished won a prize.

4. *The Class for Retarded Teen-agers and Adults*

Here is a sad and neglected group of people. God sent to our church a lovely couple with a burden for this group. They are Mr. and Mrs. Bob Houston, who say the following about their work:

A CLASS FOR RETARDED TEENS AND ADULTS

Important Needs

1. The most important need is a pastor who has a burden for the retarded and knows they need a Saviour as all of us do. Retarded people can be helped and can be brought to a saving knowledge of Jesus. A pastor who backs up the program is essential.

2. The church must be sincerely willing to provide space, equipment, and transportation to bring them in.

3. The teachers of this special class should be those who look upon these people with tender love, not pity, and see their need even when sometimes they are unlovely. The teachers must have firm discipline and order. These dear ones sense your innermost feelings and know whether you are truly sincere. We would recommend husband and wife teams if possible. Certainly you would need a man and woman, because there would be bathroom problems. Also, some of these people are large, besides being physically handicapped.

A teacher should be creative and willing to work hard. It's good for them to make Bible stories come alive. Teachers must call in each home and explain what is taught and how it is taught. It's a real pleasure to do calling and so important to do this regularly. Not all homes welcome you, however.

The teachers and helpers should have a proper understanding of and about persons who are mentally retarded before beginning the work of starting a class.

Characteristics of the Retarded

1. They are real persons (souls) with needs.
    (1) A need for "Christ" as personal Saviour.
    (2) A need for Christian growth.
    (3) A need for love and understanding.
    (4) A need for guidance spiritually and in everyday living.
2. They are different from normal persons only in the speed—
    (1) Of their ability mentally to grasp, understand and retain.
    (2) In the amount of extra patience and extra love they require.
    (3) In the short attention span before getting bored.
    (4) In the extra physical handicaps many have to cope with.
    (5) In the inability of ever being able to read or write well or at all sometimes.

Solutions to Obvious Problems

1. Never go too fast or give too much at anytime. Teaching should be done in five or six different ways never taking over ten to fifteen minutes with each method.
2. Patience and extra love is acquired from God through extra prayer all week long.
3. Use flannelgraph, filmstrips, gospel magic, object lessons, Bible games, crafts, and visual songs.
4. Regarding their physical handicaps, observe and listen, but never dwell on them. Handle the handicap normally, never building it up in any way.

5. Ask workers to help each person find the place in the Bible and hold finger on place where teacher reads. Never ask anyone to read.

Classroom Facilities

1. It's very good if possible to meet in a building apart from the church building. This enables you to bring in more Catholics and Jews.

2. You need good bathroom facilities

3. Enough room if possible where they can change from assembly room to Bible story room to refreshment and craft room.

    (1) This not only breaks up the monotony of sitting so long, for it must be remembered they are there from the beginning of Sunday school until someone comes for them after church is over.

    (2) This also later enables class members to be placed into smaller groups for Bible story time, so they may learn or be taught at their level of understanding.

A List of "Do's"

1. Always greet each person with genuine love and enthusiasm. Listen quickly to what each one has to say as you guide him to the coat rack and secretary to be registered and receive name tags. The name tags can be made from construction paper in the shape of something pertaining to that Sunday's Bible verse. The verse is usually printed on the tag and taken home by the pupil to be learned.

2. Make up copies of a schedule of what takes place from 9:20 to 9:30, 9:30 to 9:40, etc., so teachers, helpers, and class members soon learn what to expect. If a change becomes necessary, make changes slowly.

3. In the beginning all things are done together such as singing, Bible verse time, Bible story time, etc. Later when the class has grown to more than twenty in attendance, separate into advanced and slow for Bible story time only.

4. Be sure the room, equipment, and material are set up before class members arrive.

5. Be sure helpers are obtained and instructed what to do

during the week.

6. Give invitation at close of every Bible story.

7. Make arrangements for class to come into regular church services once a month thus giving the class members an opportunity to hear preaching and music and learn how to conduct themselves in church.

8. Make regular times for bathroom privileges.

A List of "Don'ts"

1. Never permit loud talking or unnecessary noise.
2. Never give more attention or friendliness to any certain few.
3. Never continually call on same ones or on the ones who know the answer.
4. Never permit anyone to leave classroom without permission and a chaperone.
5. Never permit the overactive or overly friendly to sit together.
6. Never start allowing questions to be asked loudly without raising of hand first.
7. Never permit any to have extra privileges because of ability.

Needed Equipment

1. Filmstrip machine and projector.
2. Tape recorder for class to hear themselves and do better.
3. Object lessons, books and objects for better explaining Bible words and stories.
4. Coat rack equipped for hats and boots.
5. Flannel boards for visual aids.
6. A file on each class member.
7. Large clock such as in public schools.
8. Large, long tables for refreshments and craft time.
9. Good lighting in rooms as many have bad eyes.
10. Visual backgrounds and figures of Bible stories.
11. Bus service and/or church volunteers to pick up and bring members who do not have transportation. This will account for over 75% of the members of this special class.

How to Obtain Prospects

1. Bob and I, being parents of a retarded child, were active in the Gary Council for Retarded Children. I was treasurer for two years, also room mother, and we were on many committees. I had a list of names of the Lake County Association Retarded Children and Adults. We were friends with many other parents of retarded people. This is how we got prospects first.

2. Another way is to visit such programs in your area and ask for names.

3. Parents in your own church should be of help.

4. Some hospitals now have a therapy program. One might visit and get prospects there.

5. *Unmarried Adults' Class*

Many adults never marry; others lose their mates during the early or middle years of life. Life's circumstances have led them to have different interests and ways of life than those of married people. Hence, we provide for these people a special class. I have asked their teacher, Mr. Walter Mitziga, to give his ideas and impressions about this work. He writes as follows:

Every church has a group of people to whom life has been perplexing and bewildering; people who have not found themselves in the normal social associations. These are unmarried adults from 35 years and up. Some have never married, a few are still seeking, some are widows and widowers, several have been abandoned by their mates, and a few are divorced.

In the average church these people are scattered in adult Sunday school classes—the class taught by the pastor, a Men's Brotherhood Class, a Women's Class. However, many do not attend Sunday school. Most cannot identify themselves with any particular group in the church because of their situation. These are lonely people without opportunity to fellowship with other Christians. Here is where an Unmarried Adult Sunday School Class can help in the

Sunday school.

Prospects for this class are found within the membership. Some are active, a few are active in a limited way, and several are actually backsliders. Members of the class invite friends who find themselves in the same situation in life. Our visitation people who call on prospects and visitors recommend people to this class. Friends and relatives in the church give names of prospects they think would benefit by being in such a class.

Such a class is organized with a president, vice-president and a secretary, who collects funds for birthday cards and flowers for the sick and bereaved of the class. The teacher and his wife care for the spiritual and social activities of the class. Strong direction in social activities is necessary as outside influences sometimes are exerted in the planning of social events.

Social activities are held once a month for fellowship. Once a year a dinner in a restaurant, with a banquet room for ourselves is planned, and we bring in an outside speaker. We visit museums and planetariums, take a Christmas Walk (visiting shops that sell Christmas cards and remembrances at less than a dollar), enjoy a summer picnic, take a bus trip to outlying towns, and visit each others' homes and back yards.

To stimulate interest in other folks who are not as well off as members of the class, we assist in services at the County Home once a month. Once or twice a year we also go with the young people of our church to the Pacific Garden Mission.

The class participates in the Spring and Fall contests that the entire Sunday school promotes by arranging competitive contests with other classes. We have divided the class into two groups alphabetically for contest purposes. One year everyone in the class was a contestant and was graded by points for being faithful in attendance, bringing a visitor to class, bringing a visitor to another class or department, and by making calls made on prospects given to the entire class. Every visitor to the class, every name given by friends and relatives, and every prospect on the church roll not attending Sunday school is contacted and contacted again throughout the year by different persons at different times.

6. *The Class for College Age and Unmarried Young Adults*

Many churches find that when their young people graduate from high school, they also graduate from Sunday school. Because of this, one of the most active works in First Baptist Church is the class for college-age and unmarried young adults. This often provides a bridge between high school and marriage. It is a very vital part of our church life and certainly helps us to reach many who would be unreached otherwise. This work is under the direction of Mr. John Olsen, who says the following about it:

THE COLLEGE AND PROFESSIONAL AGE CLASS

Mention the prospect of teaching a college-age class to the average Sunday school workers, and the chances are they will respond with much fear and trembling. I know! It happened to me. I had formed a mental picture of the college-age class member as one who is constantly analyzing everything a teacher says as to accuracy, logic, delivery, and grammatical errors. Actually, nothing could be farther from the truth. Teaching the college-age class has been a rewarding, vitalizing experience, and I have enjoyed every minute of it.

Why? For this reason: They are not the least bit stuffy; they act natural. To earn their confidence and respect I try to be just as natural plus genuinely friendly in return. I constantly recognize that I can learn something from each one of them. They are a storehouse of mature learning and adult knowledge. I am also aware that regardless of stature or degree of education, each one knows something and may even have a unique talent that no one else possesses. For example, at one time or another our class has included high school teachers, a student nearing his doctorate degree, an electronics engineer, automobile mechanics, construction laborers, secretaries, interior designers, theology students, a chemical engineer, sales clerks, restaurant managers, steel mill workers, and several who could barely read. I recall one fellow who was saved out of a rough, tough street gang because of a concerned Christian employer. This fellow had a talent no one else had. He was a shoemaker. He could repair shoes with a craftsman's skill. I owned several pairs of shoes of varying value. He would amuse himself and discomfit me by looking at them a short moment and telling me within a dollar or two what I paid for them. One Sunday morning I stood up to teach. Suddenly I became keenly aware that looking at me and expecting words of wisdom regarding the lesson were at least a half dozen ministerial students from nearby Moody Bible Institute, an English teacher, and one schooled in mathematics and science. My first thought was, "DON'T PANIC." Next, I applied a simple psychological help that never fails. It is based on the simple rule that EVERYBODY KNOWS SOMETHING THAT THE OTHER PERSON DOES NOT KNOW. I had studied the lesson. I had asked God for wisdom. I knew something that they didn't know—today's Sunday school lesson. Properly prepared, I had the advantage. From the vast store of knowledge within that class I would draw information. Using leading questions I would use someone's Bible knowledge or technical knowledge to verify a point, to validate an example, or to prove an illustration. It is thus that I invite class participation. Seldom do I permit lengthy presentation or discussion of an opinion regarding a point in the lesson. When I do, it must be concise, and it is used only to stimulate thinking, not to raise an issue. For example, I might ask for ideas regarding the *functional* purpose of each of the four coverings of the Tabernacle. Logical answers might be: protection, more protection, insulation, and beauty. A phrase I use often is, "Prove your statement from the Bible."

Unique Characteristics

1. *Maturity.* Though they are *young* adults they are definitely adults, and I regard them as such. They may refer to each other as "kids" in their conversation. I NEVER DO! At least, I do not intentionally. I impose a fine of $1.00 upon myself every time I refer to them as "kids." I usually address them as "ladies and gentlemen," "folks," or "young people" depending upon the situation. In deference to those who work as opposed to those attending

school we call ourselves "College and Professional Age Young Adults."

2. *Less Sophistication.* We have played games and have had amusements at some of our class socials that would shake the aplomb of the average high school student right down to his shoes. High schoolers don't want to be treated like children and thus often adopt an air of reserve. Certain activities are taboo because they might cause a loss of dignity. The college age, on the other hand, could care less as long as it's within the bounds of good taste. Can you imagine a group of college-age young people playing "hopscotch" or "jump-rope" at a summer outing? We've done it and it was fun.

This one difference between high schoolers and college age is the biggest reason why there should *never* be a combined high school and college-age group in a church. The program eventually winds up geared to the needs of the high school age, and the college age usually ends up left out and soon becomes the forgotten age group as it is in many churches today.

3. *Self-Generating.* Give them an assignment, or better, let them get an inspiration and the college-age students will generally carry it through to the end without further stimulation. Most of the banquets and programs are planned, worked up, and presented without a great deal of push from the group sponsor. As teacher/sponsor I reserve the right to be a "road-block" if need be. A planning committee will always come to me for approval. Sometimes I may modify an item or offer some suggestions. These are always accepted graciously and the work proceeds. Never once have any of the committees abandoned their projects because of a disagreement with the teacher/sponsor. Never once have I had to wield any discipline because of improper conduct at a group-sponsored activity.

4. *Rapport.* College-age folks accept each other more easily than do high schoolers. Because of this, reticent ones are less often shunned and active cliques are less of a problem than they are with older or younger groups. I am constantly on the lookout for anything remotely resembling a clique and the loner who will not initiate an acquaintance with others. To the loner I will often give little

seemingly unobtrusive jobs such as passing out songbooks or anything that will place that one in direct contact with the others. If a stranger or visitor sits by himself for more than just a minute or so before the class session starts, I will always call one of the class "regulars" outside into the hall, give them the stranger's name and some information about him and suggest that he go back in and sit near the stranger, introduce himself or herself, and strike up a conversation. If I notice a clique in the making, I will often select a clique-member to introduce himself to a stranger.

Organization

As previously mentioned, we do not have a combined high school and college-age program because of the divergent characteristics and interests of the two groups. Furthermore, our entire college-age program is unified. The teacher of the Sunday school class is also sponsor of the evening Training Union. This unification precludes any conflicting activity; the left hand always knows what the right hand is doing. Also, no college-ager need feel left out because he happens to teach a younger class or works as a departmental secretary. Any planned activity automatically includes every unmarried young adult in the church.

Once a year, in December we nominate and elect a class President and Vice-President. Those elected take office effective January first each year. Before nominations are opened I instruct the class to choose prayerfully candidates who have some ability to lead and who will have an active part in the Sunday school opening exercises. Choose candidates, I advise, who are regular in attendance and faithful to group activities. '

I reserve the privilege of selecting a class secretary/treasurer. I look for one who, again, is regular in attendance and who is apt to keeping records and properly handling the offerings. Our class has its own treasury. A checking account is kept at a local bank. All disbursements require two signatures: the secretary/treasurer's and the teacher/sponsor's.

Typical Programs

The Sunday school lesson starts promptly at 10:00 a.m. I make a point of *ALWAYS* being the first one in the classroom each Sunday morning. That way I can check on chair arrangement, draw any illustrations needed on the chalkboard and, most important, I can greet each one personally as he enters the room. I try to chat a brief moment with each person, complimenting a new dress, hairdo or suit, or commenting on recent happenings of interest to that person. These are PEOPLE we are dealing with, not just a class. Everyone thrives on recognition; individual recognition. That's the reason a warm INDI-VIDUAL greeting is most imperative. The fifteen- to twenty-minute period before the lesson is flexible. We usually sing one and sometimes two hymns or choruses. The balance of the time is used reading letters from college students and servicemen, making announcements, and introducing visitors. It is a good idea to occasionally present a vocal or instrumental group during the opening twenty-minute period.

I make much of the introduction of visitors. As they come into the classroom they fill out visitor's cards, giving their name, home address, their local address if their home is not in the local area, where they work or attend school, their phone number, and birth date. Very often I can determine something interesting about the visitor from the information on the card. For example: On September 24, 1967, we had an unusually large number of visiting students from Moody Bible Institute. I guess the bus driver steered two busloads into the college-age class. There were 51 visitors from Moody Bible Institute alone. To the utter amazement of myself and all concerned there were eight Moody students about whom I knew something. One girl was from Groton, Connecticut. Well, that's a large submarine base where the first atomic submarine was researched, developed, and constructed. Another's home was on the south side of Chicago. She was a member of a Baptist church pastored by a friend of mine of long standing. I mentioned his name and some of the things we did together years before. One student from Pekin, Illinois, was a member of Pekin Bible Church. I mentioned that his church was organized by Rev. Charles Svoboda, of the Illinois Bible Church Association, a friend from the time we attended the same college-age Sunday school class. A student from Souderton, Pennsylvania, was a member of the Grace Bible Church in Souderton. I said, "That's the church pastored by Rev. Gerald Stover, right?" I had met Pastor Stover when he had stayed in the home of my wife's parents while holding a week of meetings in their church. One girl from Crown Point, Indiana, had the same name as an auctioneer and candidate for public office that I had once met in a restaurant in Lowell, Indiana. I asked if she was related to him, and she said that he was her cousin. A Miss Elaine Taylor gave her home as Norway, Michigan. I immediately spotted a relationship. I said, "Are you related to Pastor William Taylor of Norway, Michigan, a former member of Cicero Bible Church?" A little startled, she said, "Yes, he is my father and we still hold a membership in Cicero Bible Church." Twenty years ago, when Pastor Taylor was a student at Moody Bible Institute, he and I taught classes in the same Sunday school department. When I came to the last visitor card I was absolutely astounded. I recognized a very unpronounceable name as that of a business associate of mine. The address on the card indicated a correlation. I announced the name, "Larry Mykytiuk." The fellow stood, surprised that a stranger had pronounced his name correctly, perhaps for the first time in his life. I said, "Are you related to Tom Mykytiuk, formerly a salesman for A. H. Robins Company, pharmaceutical manufacturers, who recently resigned to become a minister?" Larry, still visibly surprised, said, "Yes, he is my brother." What a day that was! The important thing was that those folks, especially, felt less like strangers because somebody knew them. As much as possible, try to say something personal to each visitor as he is introduced. I may not always reap the harvest I did on that particular Sunday morning but often there is something of interest with every visitor. It may be some interesting history or geography surrounding their home town. Mention it. Make them feel at home in your class.

The evening Training Union is 45 minutes in length.

Since about half of those who attend are also members of the adult choir, we dismiss in time for the Sunday choir practice. We devote a few minutes at the start of each Training Union session for fellowship. The programs are varied. We have had prayer meetings for the entire time; guest speakers; testimony sessions; interesting films; quizzes; and Bible studies, for either one evening or a series over several weeks. A recent series was on "How Fulfilled Bible Prophecies Validate the Veracity and Accuracy of the Bible."

The Training Union is important because it gives those who teach in various Sunday school departments in the morning a chance to co-mingle with other college-age folks in the evening.

Prospects

The greatest single number of class members come in on Promotion Day. These are the high school seniors who are graduating. Most churches traditionally observe Promotion Sunday in October each year. We did until tradition gave way to expediency. The problem which faced the college-age class was a serious one. When about half of the graduating high school seniors left in September for colleges and universities across the country, we wouldn't get to even meet them until they returned home for Christmas vacation. By that time they usually felt completely alien to the college-age class and many would fail to join in with the others. They would have to be met, be introduced, and then try to get acquainted, only to leave again in a week or ten days, never feeling as though they were definitely a part of the college-age group. Wisely, the Sunday school teachers unanimously elected to change Promotion Day to coincide with the end of the secular school year. Now the graduating seniors enter into the college-age activities three months before they leave for college and are completely assimilated before they leave.

Other prospects are brought in by class members who invite their co-workers from their places of employment. Other prospects are visitors to our church services. From their visitors' cards contact is made and they are told of a class composed of people their age with their interests at heart.

Promotional Work

We have had several contests within the class. Points were awarded for certain accomplishments such as bringing visitors, being present in class, and arriving on time. While we didn't become filled to overflowing, several people worked very hard and were awarded fine Thompson Chain Reference Bibles, and Amplified Bibles.

The most successful promotional stunt we ever had was an attendance contest held against the Couples' Class. It was successful from the standpoint that a lot of people came out to Sunday school. Yet, ironically, our Pioneer Class, who was the challenger, did not win. It all started one evening during the height of one of our seasonal Sunday school attendance campaigns when one of the Pioneer Class members overheard a Couples' Class member state that we would not make our quota on our "Big Day." Of course, we took this as a friendly insult. We immediately drew up a set of resolutions and presented a challenge to the Couples' Class. The winning class, according to the challenge, was to be treated to a $12.50 "Tornado" sundae at the Melody Lane Restaurant by the losers, and the losers' class president and teacher were to receive a whipped cream pie tossed into their faces by the winning team. In our haste to challenge the Couples' Class we failed to establish ground rules and take several things into consideration. (1) We failed to realize that the Couples' Class gets their prospects by two's — a man and his wife — whereas the Pioneer Class gets their prospects one at a time because they are single. (2) We failed to establish whether the winner would be determined by a numerical superiority or by the highest percentage over their quota figure. The result was that on the deciding day the Pioneer Class had one hundred five in attendance (their all-time record) against the Couples' Class attendance of an even one hundred. However, since the Couples' Class had a smaller quota, they were easily the winners on a percentage over quota basis. The promotion was far from being a failure as far as people were concerned for many people came out to

Sunday school who would not otherwise have come. On the day of the pay-off, or more literally, PIE-off, the Pioneer Class drove the Couples' Class by bus to the Melody Lane Restaurant for the Tornado sundae — two and one half gallons of ice cream resplendent with whipped cream and appropriately delivered with sparklers sparkling, sirens blowing, cymbals clanging and all the hoopla that went with it. Later that evening back at the church, the teacher and president of the Pioneer Class donned plastic bags that covered all but their heads and stood with the solemnity of Stephen the martyr while C. W. Fisk, teacher of the Couples' Class plopped two juicy whipped cream pies right in their faces.

Perhaps we will never know until we reach Heaven the real outcome of that contest measured in the number of people that came out to Sunday school and the number of souls won to Jesus as a result.

It was fun.   But, the next time we challenge a class we will make certain that they are not married!

Activities

Something always seems to be going on with the college-age group. Basically, our activities fall into the five following categories: Sunday morning breakfasts, Sunday evening "Take-overs," Saturday socials, outings, and banquets.

Two or three times a year we will have a Sunday morning breakfast. The purpose, as with all of our activities, is to provide fellowship, heeding the admonition of Romans 12:10, *"Be kindly affectioned one to another with brotherly love; in honour preferring one another."*

We generally serve coffee, milk, orange juice, and a large variety of rolls and doughnuts. No chairs are set up in order to preserve an atmosphere of informality. We allow about a half hour for breakfast. During this time we may have a few choruses, and we make the announcements and introduce any new people. The lesson starts promptly at the usual time as the class takes seats in a random fashion.

A "Take-over" is a name that was coined when we separated from the high school department. Originally, a

"Take-over" corresponded with a high school "Sing." In effect, and, of course, in a very spiritual manner we "Take-over" the Church Fellowship Hall, a corner of a restaurant, or someone's home for what we call fellowship, fun, and food.   There is no set pattern.   Very often we will have a "Take-over" very spontaneously with no more than several hours' notice.   We will order pizza or hamburgers and have them ready for pick-up or delivery by the time the Sunday evening church service ends.   Most often we will sing, have some testimonies, a prayer time, and a devotional.   A "Take-over" is always planned when someone leaves for the Armed Service or when someone comes home on leave.   These, of course, are planned "Take-overs."   They will most often be in the Fellowship Hall or someone's home.   Sometimes we will invite a guest speaker for the devotional.   Always, the person involved is the guest of honor.   Recently, as one of the fellows left for the Army, we had a "Take-over" entitled, "This is Your Life, Johnny Mark," outlining various high points in John Mark's life and each was dramatized in an appropriately comical episode.   Several weeks later another, Mark Graves, was being drafted. Mark was our gourmet. His talent is out-eating everybody else.   Mark also comes from a large family.   The theme of the "Take-over" was "food."   One game was a food-eating relay.   The high point was an hilarious portrayal of the hazards involved in eating under crowded conditions dramatized by Mark and his brother Jeffrey.

The food cost at our "Take-overs" is covered through voluntary contributions from those present. We total the cost of the food, divide by the number present and announce the average cost.   No set amount is ever required, just in case anyone may be suffering a temporary financial setback.

Another activity is our Saturday social. Sometimes we have Friday night socials.   There are at least two good bowling lanes in our area where we can bowl in good taste in a comparatively refined atmosphere. An evening of bowling may be followed by refreshments and fellowship in someone's home. One time we went to a very old farm-house converted into a place that serves a large variety of unusual pancakes.   One recent Saturday social was a

Treasure Hunt. We met at the church at 7:30 p.m. and divided into six teams of three and four each. Each team was given a set of sealed directions to follow. There were about eight destinations in each set of directions. Each group had to first interpret the directions, then find the destinations, and then determine what to do once they got there. The final destination awarded amusing prizes to the winning team, and a lavish chicken buffet supper was served to all.

Outings are always on Saturday because of the longer time involved. Places we have gone include Brookfield Zoo, the Chicago Police Crime Laboratory, several museums, and the Adler Planetarium to view a presentation entitled, "The Star of Bethlehem."

"A Day at Naomi Wedding's Farm" is always unforgettable. Naomi, one of our group, lives on a farm about thirty miles south of Hammond. For the past two years we have had outings there. We arrive there between two and three in the afternoon. A typical sequence of activity is as follows: softball game, watermelon feed, tug-o'-war, treasure hunt, dodge-ball, egg toss, volley ball, some less active contests, supper, and more games. Gallons of ice cold punch are always available. After dark we gather around a large campfire to roast marshmallows, sing choruses, give some testimonies, and close with a devotional. We end the day bone weary and sometimes a little damaged. One fellow earned the name "Cowboy" Douglas after he was thrown by an uncooperative pony.

Twice a year we have a banquet. Usually these are held in August, just before school begins, and in December, right after Christmas. The ingenuity of a college-ager is totally revealed at a banquet. One summer they had a South Sea Island motif. Dan Johnson and several others constructed a lagoon about 25 feet long and six feet wide, complete with live fish! The supports in the banquet room became palm trees, and there were flowers everywhere. Where did the flowers come from? You would never guess! Barbara Mark discovered that funeral homes discard most of the flowers after a funeral. The banquet committee called all the local funeral homes and just plain asked for the flowers. They got them. I will confess to feeling a little vulturous as I drove down streets looking for funeral processions to determine at what funeral homes the flowers might be obtained.

The food for our banquets is either catered or prepared by certain women of the church. At one of the most successful banquets, however, the fellows prepared everything and the food was actually delicious. Tom Beilby prepared the roast and a very tasty salad dressing. Canned foods were disallowed, and Arnold Johnson concocted a soup that was the best I had ever tasted. It was the first time in his life he had cooked anything. The mashed potatoes were excellent though a little gray and slightly lumpy. We accused John Flasman of mashing them with his bare feet. Jeff Graves supervised the Parker House rolls. Terry Cunningham and Dave Quigg collaborated on the pie and homemade ice cream. All the fellows had a hand in the tossed salad. It was a most wonderful dinner.

Christmas week of 1967 we held our first banquet in the Fellowship Hall of our new Sunday school building. The committee discussed at long length various possible table arrangements. The arrangement agreed upon permitted every table to be near the focal point of skits and presentations. The committee asked me to preside as Master of Ceremonies. I make a habit of preparing more than is needed in case of anything unforeseen. After several skits and musical selections went off very well, I announced that we would present "Table Talent." In five minutes I would begin picking tables to present a skit, a song, or anything they could prepare in five minutes. The results were "side-splitting." One was a fractured, off-key quartet where one member seemed to be fighting off waves of nausea and finally fainted. Another skit depicted a scene in a doctor's reception room where one poor patient was absorbing all the symptoms of the other patients. The rest were equally funny. Miss Pat Webb and those who work with her to develop interesting programs and "Take-overs" have done much to make a sponsor's job easier.

A college-age characteristic I didn't mention in the beginning deserves special attention. That is appreciation. Our folks have expressed gratitude in many ways. Greatest of all was February 20, 1968. It was our 25th wedding anniversary.

We expected to spend a quiet evening at home with a few visiting relatives. About 7:30 p.m. an avalanche of college-age folks overwhelmed us bearing food, gifts, and all the entertainment. Naturally we were touched and overjoyed beyond words.

I guess I am partial to the college-age department. The college-ager is a pleasure to work with and to be with. You may wonder, "Is it hard work?" Sometimes. "Is it time-consuming?" Yes, and there is lots of study involved. "Is it discouraging?" Never, except where it pertains to my own failings, but every once in a while a young man or young lady will come up to me at the close of the Sunday school hour and say, "That was a good lesson, Mr. Olsen." I know they are sincere and not perfunctory and I am warmed. I thank them verbally, and deep down inside I say, "Thank you, Lord, for college-agers."

7. *The Class for Poor Children*

This is a class that meets at noon on Sunday. It is attended by children who normally would not attend Sunday school. They come from poor areas, and many of them do not have a decent meal all week. We provide a warm meal for them and teach them the Word of God. This class is directed by Mr. John Colsten, our Rescue Mission superintendent. His remarks concerning this work follow:

MISSION CLASS

The First Baptist Church has a work among the under-privileged children of the neighboring area. This is an extension of our Sunday school work.

The class meets on Sunday afternoon and utilizes the facilities of the church. Because the class meets on Sunday afternoon, it is possible to reach children who because of shabby clothing would not come or be allowed to come to regular Sunday school. Also it is possible to reach those who may attend church elsewhere.

The class is promoted by advertising. A poster in a place where many children pass by during the week is effective.

A mailing list is helpful also, and ditto reminders about coming events can be sent to them. Every child likes to receive mail. Personal contact with children in the area is the best method for getting the children to come. Initially, I went into the residential area with bubble gum and a mimeographed flyer on the day before I first had the class. There were 53 present the first Sunday, and it grew in attendance to over 90. Sometimes a little gift or treat is given. We have also had a ventriloquist, magician, and a strong man for an extra treat for the children.

The class begins at 1:30 p.m. The first fifteen minutes of the class is conducted on a Sunday school assembly basis. The Sunday school lesson is then taught and many times an invitation is given in order to reach the unsaved.

At about 2:15 p.m. a hot lunch is served. We alternate basically between two different meals: Hot dogs, baked beans, potato chips, cookies, and juice or milk are served one Sunday. The following Sunday we serve "Sloopy Joes," potato chips (or cheeze-flavored corn puffs), whole kernel corn, cookies, and juice or milk. For some of the children, it is the only decent meal they get all week.

These children, of course, come from some poor backgrounds. They should be handled in a disciplined way. It may be their only opportunity for learning proper behavior. They should also be loved. Again, it may be their only opportunity for real love.

Hence, all ages in all walks of life may find those of like interest in the Sunday school of First Baptist Church. Let us forget no one in our attempt to reach people for Christ.